M000024256

sidetracked

sidetracked

AMANDA MAILEY

Copyright © 2020 by Amanda Mailey

All rights reserved. No part of this book may be reproduced or transmitted in any form or by any means, electronic or mechanical, including photocopying, recording, or by any information storage and retrieval system without the written permission of the author, except where permitted by law.

ISBN 978-1-09831-494-1

All photographs are courtesy of the author.

Cover design by Tian Mulholland.

Referenced on Page 104
Whitehead, Dan (2018). 'Sophisticated' Albanian gangs liked to people trafficking surge in UK. Accessed through https://news.sky.com/story/sophisticated-albanian-gangs-linked-to-people-trafficking-surge-in-uk-11555887

Referenced on Page 174
ExploringMacedonia.com (2018). EM / Got to / Cities / Ohrid. Accessed through *http://www.exploringmacedonia.com/ohrid.nspx*

Referenced on Page 177-178
LonelyPlanet.com (2018). Europe / North Macedonia / Lake Ohrid / Attractions. Accessed through https://www.lonelyplanet.com/macedonia/attractions/museum-on-water-bay-of-bones/a/poi-sig/1544350/360131

Referenced on Page 206
Zarya, Valentina (2018). The Share of Female CEOs in the Fortune 500 Dropped by 25% in 2018. Accessed through https://fortune.com/2018/05/21/women-fortune-500-2018/

When risking it all, in a quest to find joy in the art of living, comes at just the right time.

In the wake of Trump's presidency, the #metoo movement, emboldened racism, gun violence rising, three layoffs in five years, and the height of commercialism, this successful ad executive has had enough. Spirit dampened, with mostly anger where there once was laughter, she risks it all in search of a more meaningful connection with herself, her family, and the world.

Set in her hometown of the PNW and the unfamiliar lands of Albania, she recounts her personal experience in an honest portrayal of self-discovery reflecting on mainstream American cultural norms and expectations. Knowing nothing about Tirana, Albania when she arrives, her observations of these two societies surface a new awakening. Get lost reading her intimate thoughts as she struggles to heal by hitting the reset button.

For my husband and kids.
Sean, Jackson and Isabel, thank you for the opportunity to find my way.

Preface

I was born on April 21, 1979. I am the second child, first daughter, born in my mixed family of four sisters and two brothers. My mother is a middle-child raised in a white Catholic family with seven kids in Buffalo, NY. My father is the youngest-child raised in an Ilocano-Filipino farming family with four kids in San Martin, CA. Besides his older brother, my dad and other siblings are first generation American-born. When my mom came to live with her brother in Alaska in her early 20s, she met my dad when he was playing and touring with his band at the time. She and my older brother moved to California with him, the two married and I was their first child. My parents divorced when I was five years old and my mom moved us to Oregon with her boyfriend, who she married and had my youngest brother. My dad remained in California where he, too, remarried and had my youngest sister. This is how my story started. It's a series of choices made and distances traveled by my parents that created the world and family I grew up in.

It's July 2018. At 39 years old, I live in NE Portland, Oregon. I have put my demanding 16 year marketing career on hold to travel distances with my husband, son, and daughter to seek out a new way of living in Tirana, Albania. From day one, I've been a curious observer with constant self-reflection. As I was going through the motions of adulthood, something felt off. I was having more questions than answers. There was distance in my relationships, buried trauma in my past, and life priorities weren't quite right. This book holds a collection of personal observations and reflections over 100 days of my choice to reach for better. It's an experience that will forever leave an imprint on my family's life. I hope my own struggle, contemplation, and passion for change will inspire others to assess and realign their life with their heart, if it's not there. Because we all get sidetracked time-to-time.

Acknowledgements

I would like to acknowledge and thank Shannon Kerry and Bobby Hart. Not only are they close friends I made on this adventure, but they also generously offered to act as my editors.

Special thank you to my beta readers and to my family and friends who supported me in publishing my first book.

Contents

sidetracked

Chapter 1

The world can't stop, but you can.

* Day 1 *

The Monday after I quit my job. No alerts. No work email. No work IMs. No work social posts to check or respond to. The quiet makes me a bit sad. Like the world is leaving me out. I keep getting the feeling I'm forgetting something; that I'm unproductive. Being on hand, when needed, has been my life for the last 16 years. Mobile phone glued to my side. This was my purpose. The "always on" digital culture was expected. Constant noise with no questions asked. Vacation time may be the only time a shutdown is acceptable. Out of office is turned on, but there is still the quick scan of the emails coming in. If I do resist checking work email, the personal side of my life creeps in. The expectation to document and tell everyone what I'm doing while on vacation. Pictures, stories, videos, the whole play-by-play to fill the feeds of social media. My followers get to come with me without actually coming with me. This way of life has made my mind tired and my spirit dampened. Burned out. Like being "online" is the only way to be connected to others. I'm in search of a new connection. Time for a change. Wait. My co-workers just sent me a text saying hello. That was nice. Baby steps.

* Day 2 *

What better way to break from it all than head to the beach. The long Oregon coastline, with its famous stacked ocean boulders and dune grass, is different than the tropical or warmer climate beaches. Windless days are rare and you're thankful if the sun is out, but it's peaceful regardless. Sometimes you wait for the zipper cloud to do its thing to unveil the yellow ball in the sky just in time for the evening sunset. You take nothing for granted. Everything is a gift of pure circumstance, but somehow feels magical. It's my happy place. Something about the sea air and the sound of the ocean takes this high-strung woman down a few notches, but I couldn't live full-time in these smaller coastal towns. My body and personality are wired to slow down only temporarily or it will self-combust. I live for the life that needs rest and recovery. A classic cause and effect, yin and yang for true balance. As much as I love the downtime, especially the way the scenery and mood are different from my up time, the thrill ride is an addiction.

Highlights from today: 21 Dungeness crab were caught after a 48-hour pacific ocean soak in my father-in-law's crab pots; I played in town with the kids while the pots were retrieved; fireworks purchased for tomorrow's main event; Jazzy dog and I made it out on the beach for a stroll along the water. Today, I was a professional dog walker and crab cracker. Actually, I'm not a professional anything.

* Day 3 *

A couple of days at the beach, turns you introspective. The sound of the ocean and sea air must do that to anyone I would think. Back at home, about 20 years of "stuff" has been purged and yet everyday there seems to be more to do. Selling what's left is a chore.

1. Stage item.
2. Photograph item.
3. Measure item.
4. Research item's market value.
5. Cry about how cheap you're selling item.
6. Write Craigslist ad for item.
7. Answer questions about item; stupid questions for something you are selling for $10.
8. Explain how item received scratch.
9. Arrange for item to be purchased.
10. Host a stranger on your front porch to pick up item.
11. Watch as they look over item and prepare their speech to low ball you.
12. Hold out hand for cold hard cash for item.
13. Shut the door behind you and never see item again.
14. Press delete on the conversation in your phone about item.
15. Expire the item's ad on Craigslist.
16. Notify others that have inquired about item.
17. Start all over again.

50+ more items to go.

Perhaps this is my routine for this transitional period. If it is, it helps to think we aren't erasing what was, but instead making room for much more. The whole thought is easier to stomach as I witness another coastal sunset on the horizon. It, too, is in transition and it's beautiful. The way the wispy clouds trace across creates an incredible depth to the open sky. The backdrop is a deep blue moving through different shades with each passing second as it reflects what's left of the light. A strip of orange and pink hues hover over the water, which draws attention to the transition point. The waves, slowly washing over the sand at low tide, invite my gaze to soften while last week's highlights run through my head.

I said "last day goodbyes" at my seventh company in my marketing career. Is that a lot? Eh. 16 years. Each turn taught me more. This last one especially revealed capabilities I didn't know I had, but I'm ready. If I had roots in something great, I would have never left. I would have never sought it out. Well maybe not never, but not at this point in our lives. Timing feels right. For the kids. For us. For me.

* Day 4 *

My body likes to wake at 8am. No matter what time I go to bed my eyes find the clock and it's 8 am again. Waking up without the interruption of a blaring alarm clock starts the day right. No jolting of the body when it goes off. My eyes open up slowly when they want to. Dreams aren't cut short. My heart rate isn't racing from the scare of the loud beeping. I typically wouldn't call myself a morning person. I immediately notice a difference in my mood. The muscles in my face stay stretched out instead of being all squished up at the sign of light. I have a new urge to make my bed and I'm not gunning for the coffee. I will need to get myself up earlier in the future. See the sunrise and move my body. But for now, this is nice.

Other observations. I'm already finding more appreciation for cooking. Fingers smell like garlic and chopping is meditative. Cooking not because I have to and instead because I want to is a simple yet appealing shift. Real butter on toast with strawberry preserve is a rediscovered treat. Evening sunsets are family entertainment. 2012 wine bottles are being pulled out of our wine cellar aka basement. When we bought and stored the bottles, I had no idea we'd one day celebrate a bunch of "lasts" in Oregon with a raised glass from these NW vineyards. Lastly, updating my LinkedIn Profile wasn't that scary. It's officially out there, professionally. I'm on a break.

* Day 5 *

Insomnia strikes. I've been tossing and turning over "the list" for the last hour and a half. All the big stuff is done or on its way to being done. Now the small stuff. It's like a wedding or big event. Don't get overconfident when there are check marks on the music, catering, dress, and wedding site. The little stuff can kill ya. All the tiny but important things are running through my head. Time to make yet another list for my life. Isn't that what control freaks do? Lists calm AND drive us nuts. Writing it down, getting it out of my head, does help. Once I start the list, things randomly hit my brain mid-sentence or if I see some sign on the road, I recall another thing I need to add to it. Thank you, Google Docs and mobile phone for always being by my side.

On the goodbye tour, we've left the beach and made our way to the desert for Jackson's baseball tournament. The house is out of sight, but not fully out of mind. The dry land vegetation and hot temperatures have me a little out of my body. Like being drugged. Everything is heightened. Senses on overload. Everywhere I turn is some "momentous" thing. On alert, I notice when the winds change. The sound of the tree branches swaying. Colors are brighter. Flowers are in bloom everywhere. The sun sets in a fiery orange here with mountain peaks over 10,000 feet spaced out in the distance. Cacti cast shadows in the foreground. I watch all the shifts in the sky over a 30-min period like I've never seen it before. I get sad when the colors dissipate to black. I drag Jazzy home in the dark. Neither of us wants to go back in the house.

* Day 6 *

The look on people's faces continues. We have a pretty solid streak of confused expressions reflecting back at us when we tell them where we're moving. I admit I still can't say it with a straight face either and then there's my inflection when I spit out "Albania" like it's a question. This mini-vacation road tripping Oregon, has us roaming like nomads, but it's temporary. We'll be back in our Portland home in the next few days and then hopping a plane in the next few weeks. Selling off everything, besides the house, and moving the family out of the country for the next three years is hard to make sense of, but I knew we'd do this someday. Well, I hoped we would. I've been searching for the feeling we had when we were 21/22 years old living in Ireland and then backpacking all over Europe. As a couple and then as a family we've traveled internationally quite a bit over the last 15 years or so, but it's not the same and it is incredibly costly as a family of four now. I feel like we're running out of time to see all corners of the world. The urgency driving this jump-in-with-both-feet gesture as we turn 40 has me excited. I want to inhabit a new way of living. A non-American way of living. I say this not to be a snob and denounce where I am from, but there are lots of routines, spaces, and traditions to share in; to make them a part of you. I don't believe we are meant to live our life in one way. Sure, your everyday bubble is pretty small when you think of it. The world is filled with 7.6 Billion people, 7 continents, and 195 countries, but most of our life is spent in a 20-mile diameter around our home. Widen that aperture. The Maileys are ready to explore.

* Day 7 *

It's settling in. I left my job. I am not on PTO right now. I'm on a work sabbatical. Unemployed. Semi-retired. Hiatus. What do I call this? And the crazy thing is I don't know when I will start again. Working has been so much of my identity. As long as I can remember, I wanted to work. Starting with babysitting at 9 or 10 years old, then mowing lawns, then working at the dance studio, then Intel, then the advertising agency circuit, then director of marketing of a startup. To me, work meant I had money and money equals independence. To need nobody. My terms. A way I liked to lead my life.

39 years old and my household income will now come solely from my husband's wages. Something I vowed never to do. But I've learned if you build a life to do it alone, you will end up that way. I trust Sean. It's time to hand over the alpha dog reins for a while. Take a break. I've had a 401K since I was 19, hefty life insurance policies and IRAs established at 29, and a home that has doubled in equity. I prepared for this moment without even knowing it. It's not all for retirement. Mid-career gap year(s) are also important when you come out of the college gates with such tenacity. I expended so much energy in things, experiences, people that left me feeling empty. Because I was doing what others and society guided me to do rather than looking inside myself. You don't know any better at a younger age. But now I know something is off. Like I've been sidetracked from where my life is supposed to be. Today, I'm pushing my reset button.

When I share we're leaving the country because Sean got an international job, people are lost when I tell them I have no plan for me. I really don't. I searched a bit online and there are reputable agencies in town. My past company even said they'd entertain the idea of me consulting from Albania if I'd be open to it. I have this opportunity and I don't want to squander it. Three years and my income is not needed for us to live. Making career choices without being money motivated is an interesting predicament to be in. Especially for someone like me. Many families live on one income. We just never have. I don't have a plan. Part of that is on purpose and part of that is just not having a clue. What I am sure of is my wants. I want to assimilate there, friends made by me and not just inherited from Sean. I want to be creative. I want to make a difference somehow. The details are to be determined. Amanda TBD.

* Day 8 *

Finishing up our Oregon road trip today, means we're in the final push to get to Albania. 22 days away before we get on our flight. I'm no longer working and Sean will stay in his current role until we leave. That means 100% "project: get us ready" is on me. Honestly, I've been in this project for the last five months, but this is the final stretch. And then there's the packing. The packing is the worst part. Restricting yourself to one 27-gallon storage crate and one carry on suitcase is hardly enough room. Each of us gets less than your standard garbage can to fill. Talk about minimalist living. I really don't want to think about it. Camping in the desert the last few days meant I've been without cell service. Felt good to shut it off. But now it's time to get back to reality.

Chapter 2

We become where we place our focus.

* Day 9 *

Moving preparations start up again. Sold off Jackson's bed. The house is beginning to look bare. With Joan's boxes making their way in, the home definitely looks like it's in transition. Contractors are back to work on home improvements and I'm making décor choices on a home that will no longer be mine. Lots of emotions flowing. Helps and hurts to see happy smiles of people walking away with items I purchased to make a home for our family. Nine sales so far and the quest continues to sell it all. It feels like monopoly money too because cash coming in is going right into the hands of the contractors. But I am comforted knowing parts of the life we built here are flowing out and into the neighborhood we have called home.

* Day 10 *

Interviewing potential renters for the house is challenging. I can't see anyone else living in our house. Not even Joan, even though she's my mother-in-law. With all the changes, it's starting to feel like a different home though. I can't believe the progress on the basement. In the past, we toyed with the idea of remodeling and hosting a student to stay with us since we live a few blocks from a University. Then kids happened and there went our time and energy. The square footage simply sat unused for years. Now we're transforming it into a short-term rental. It has been a huge undertaking, but the end is in sight and I can't wait to see it all come together. I am feeling better and better about the decision to keep the home. It could be a good source of income for us and I know it will continue to grow in value.

Owning a home is a huge milestone. I am fortunate to have owned two so far. Buying where we did, for both places, were smart and calculated decisions even though we were 20-somethings. Both areas were on the cusp of change. The wealth we will continue to gain makes our decision, of me taking time off work, feel more doable. And it gives us stability in an investment that will pay dividends for our family. Still, opening up the home to others feels foreign, but I know it's the best decision.

* Day 11 *

Even though I had a vacation, I feel drained. As if nearly 6 months of preparation and planning wasn't enough, the execution is proving to be the toughest job of my life. Many of my career skills have been transferable in this endeavor, but undertaking something that is for your family is much harder emotionally than hitting some profit margin for a company. Who knew that undoing one way of living to take on another one would be so daunting? Plus I am living where I work. It's hard to stop at the end of the day. My can-do attitude is pushing me to my limits. I know it will all be worth it. I know I can't quit now. We've come too far. The absence of all this is only weeks away, but it feels unattainable.

* Day 12 *

Spending more time at home and not the typical 9-5 in an office makes you see the world a little differently. In a neighborhood of growth, hardhats are everywhere and I share the line at the coffee shop with the framer, cement mixer, flagger, and general contractor. As the cars pull out to head into the office, the construction vans pull in. Landscaping trucks, with tons of equipment in tow, swoop in and the sound of lawn mowers echoes in the neighborhood. Housecleaner cars pull up and drag the mops, buckets, and rags to make the homes look tidy and welcoming for when the owners return. I swear I feel like I'm in a movie. It's pretty choreographed. I take my dog to the park and it's filled with stay-at-home moms and dads, bartenders and cooks, groups of summer camps, and grandparents pushing their grandkids in baby swings. There is a healthy amount of yoga pants, Starbucks cups, tattoos, cigarette smoking, that one guy that can't leave his laptop at home, and too much fingering-of- the-phone humanity. This is a scene I don't usually see when I'm out and about from 6-9pm in my neighborhood. I suppose the world takes shifts. I wonder how Albania daytime walkers spend their time.

* Day 13 *

Jackson's playing in his last baseball tournament. This weekend they battle for the 10U state championship. I have a hard time watching without getting sad. He loves the sport. And when he makes an incredible play, like sliding over home plate and barely squeaking by as "safe," I can't help but feel a little bad. He won't have this team he's grown up playing with the last three years. He'll find another team to be a part of, but there's no baseball in Albania. There will be so much he will gain living internationally, but there is no question there are things he will miss out on. The friends, the family, the good ol' American traditions, the familiar foods, his home, and looking around seeing people who look and talk like him. He just turned 11. He'll be 14 when he returns. I can only hope that he falls in love with something there like he's done here. I guess only time will tell. He's a resilient kid. Kind. Thoughtful. But uncomfortable in new situations. This will strengthen that weakness - or it could have the opposite effect. He retreats inward, like me, when he feels out of place. Making it even more important for me to help him pull through and soak up all that will be coming from every direction. A parenting challenge I willingly accept because learning these coping skills as an adult is rough. Just ask me.

* Day 14 *

Time for another break. The kids are with grandma and we are going out with many of our closest friends. Under a huge oak tree, we get to enjoy a farm-to-table meal on Sauvie Island. I love oak trees. They remind me of roaming my Filipino grandma Eufrosina Mallare's farm in California when I was a kid. I would climb and climb. The view and quiet was my escape from younger siblings that didn't want to climb as high. The sprawling branches provide tremendous shade. Hot, exposed, flat, dirt fields had the sun's intensity chasing us into the trees.

We pull up in our Lyft, with dust in our trail. The scene is out of a magazine. With everyone capturing moment-to-moment of their day for all the world to see and follow, the attention to being picturesque is amplified. It's the details. White tablecloth on long wooden tables, fresh wildflower centerpieces, handwritten chalk menu, and golden sun lighting. Perfection. A wine bottle of rosé is opened and we stroll over to an appetizer spread designed as a visual feast even before tasting. Wild daisies and dandelions frame the food. Raw colorful veggies, cured meats, melty brie, green olives, almonds, savory gazpacho topped with bay shrimp, blueberries, crusty breads, pâté, and different fruit preserves for lots of spreading. This is enough for me. A pescatarian's foodie heaven. Seconds please. Oh, and more rosé.

Sitting on a hay bale with a draped blanket, I realize I've known some of these people since 4th grade. We're grown up. Getting together is a rarity. Once a year is a miracle. And when we do have gatherings, they are mild. Not a lot of the wild. Not a lot of the letting go. They are quick and then everyone rushes home to relieve babysitters. Moments when crazy stories are born are few and far between. Tonight, was different. Guards were let down. Wives weren't eye rolling the husbands. Laughter was nonstop. I felt young again. I needed that.

* Day 15 *

Jackson cried today. Baseball ended and the finality of it all made him cry. It hurt to see him slumped over with his fingers in his eyes to wipe the tears as they streamed out. I started to cry, grandma Joan cried, other parents cried, some of the other boys cried. It broke my heart. Standing there, sweating from the 100-degree summer heat holding the lawn chairs we use at every game, I doubted. Are we making the right decision? Taking him from all this won't mess him up, right? The boys then jumped in a nearby river to cool down and the mood was lightened. To distract him, we went out to dinner and a movie after the game. Everything was happy again, until it wasn't. Putting him to bed, he sobbed. He called for me. I consoled him the best I could. I said what I could with as much confidence as I could conjure up. I can't lie to him though. I don't know what will come of all this, but I squeezed him tight until he calmed down. I told him of the friends I visited with last night; who I've known since I was his age. It made staying in touch seem possible to Jackson. Distance or not, you can keep a bond. I need to find a way to keep a bridge to these friends for him. Thank goodness for the internet and the invention of video chat. His childhood relationships can't end when we leave.

* Day 16 *

I know I'm out of work, but at the end of these preparation days I am completely spent. Balancing all these contractors is absolutely nuts. Just when I think it's under control there is a change. Timelines slip in product availability, contractors don't show up when they say they will, coordinating all the dependencies, it's a lot of work. And the dumb "little stuff" list. It's like quicksand. Cross something off, think of something else to add. Thank goodness for the few yoga and dance classes I can sprinkle in. They are helping me keep my sanity. Well, that and booze. 16 more days. Will we make it? Tomorrow I'm hitting up the day spa. Using the Mother's Day gift certificate and boy do I need it. As I type this, I am sitting on my comfy couch. It's going tomorrow. Sold to a foster parent. Another piece of Mailey furniture finding a new home.

* Day 17 *

Spa day. I slip on a red summer dress and get the kids off to soccer camp. I know the list is long, but time for myself is important. Shut off from everything for a few hours. In all the busy, it's hard to find a moment to process what's happening. Plus, I strained my back moving Jackson's bed and dresser down the stairs for our happy buyers. The dangers of Craigslisting. This deep tissue massage should help. Of course, right afterwards I will head to Home Depot to buy more items for the house, but hitting pause on it all, for even just a moment, feels good and necessary.

It's so quiet. Soothing music playing. The lights are dimmed. My heartbeat slows. Tension held in my muscles start to release as my masseuse applies plenty of pressure. I'm silent, but I catch myself crying. The world has stopped rotating. I am still. I give into her as she pushes my body around. I'm trying to be strong. Held together. But not here. Here, I just let go. 60 minutes, I surrender. Wishing it went on longer, I grab a glass of water, clear my head, and prepare for my facial. Time to add moisture back into my skin. Make me glow again. I inhale the scents. Aromatherapy with a humidifier fills up the room as she paints on my mask. The rough towel rubbed across my skin removes the heaviness from the past few months. It's like I've shed in some way. I sit up and there is a lightness. Last but not least, I'm escorted to another room for a milk foot bath with honey. My hands cupping a warm cup of tea, I sit. Soaking. Yay for this day. The bath starts to get cold. A woman kneels in front of me and begins to wash my feet. Something feels ceremonial about it.

To make the time even more well spent, I head to one of my favorite spots that happens to be down the street; a French bakery with the best nicoise salad, coffee, and pastry selection in town. It's a place I go to feel like I'm out of the country for a little bit. Sometimes when I sit at their bar area that faces the wood oven they bake in, I luck out and get to watch them make bread. Everything is so clean and scheduled and precise. The flour thrown around sets a mood, a look. Life with a dreamy filter. It's satisfying to watch. Today, no bread making but a visit to remember nonetheless. I wonder where I will sit in Albania to feel like I am at home for a bit.

Chapter 3

We are a patchwork of the people we meet.

* Day 18 *

Saying goodbye to people is the hardest part. I am up at 4am because the process is making it difficult to sleep. I believe we will be back after 3 years, but I don't know for certain. And even if we are, our community of people might not stay in Portland. We'll come back to visit, but you can't possibly see everyone in such short windows of time. The whole thing hangs on me like a wet blanket. Living here, I didn't see these people nearly enough. Life makes you choose. The routine of everyday life only has enough room. I am thankful and grateful for the communities I've been a part of, the relationships built, the people who know me. I wish I could fast forward and see us all back together again after the three years are done. To know this isn't goodbye, but instead see you later. A girl can wish.

* Day 19 *

The purging continues. Digging through boxes of stuff I forgot I had, I went down memory lane. I cried and held tight to some things while letting a few things go. 40 years on this earth can start to show in the stuff you hoard. And I'm a true consistent purger, but mostly of the kids' things or other household items. Cardboard boxes from layoffs and company exits have collected over time. I didn't want to deal with it. The pain was too great. Now I'm confronted with going through each and consolidating. Old college charcoal drawings from art class, relics from past relationships, letters from friends, years all shoved away in boxes and hidden in the many nooks and crannies of our house. Even boxes from my childhood, which were dropped off by my mom years ago, weren't sifted through until now. Sweet Valley high paperbacks and a shirt embroidered with "Most Likely to Succeed" on the breast pocket have thoughts of "why did she keep all this stuff" mixed in with "I can't believe I still have this." I sit on the floor of Jackson's bedroom in the middle of 30 years of my past littered everywhere. Holding an old letter, I look up with tears in my eyes and see Sean standing over me with a judging face. I've been up here for hours. The scene didn't look like progress, but to me it was.

Nonetheless there is more to do in our day. The rest will have to wait. Dusting myself off, I head downstairs to join the family. It's time to sell off the cars. Within a few hours, both of our cars sold and we actually made some cash on them. Bit by bit our assets (not knowing the value) continue to pay out for us. I do love our cars. I feel like we'd still pick the same cars when we come back. As an adult, sharing most everything of your life with your husband and kids, your car becomes the only thing that's really yours. It reminds me of when I coveted my bedroom as a kid. It represents me. When I'm in it, I feel independent. I barely drive, but having a car has some psychological impact too. Ownership. The freedom to jump in whenever to go where ever. It's silly, but I'll miss my blue MINI. Tomorrow, I'll be using a rental car for the last two weeks we're here. Then carless in Albania for who knows how long.

Have I mentioned that I'm exhausted? Working on all this from the moment I wake until the point I go to bed has me both physically and mentally broken. I can't wait for the pure relief of being on the other side of this mountain I've been climbing.

* Day 20 *

With two weeks left, we hand over the keys to our cars. After shopping them around three different lots, the GM car dealership bought both of our cars with the highest bid. We signed the paperwork last night and shook hands. We told our sales guy we needed one more night with them and he was fine with it. I found a bed set for the short-term rental and we needed Sean's suburban to grab it. Plus, I wanted one more night. It all happened so fast. We honestly didn't think it would happen in a day.

With all that behind us, we showed up to GM this morning with both cars cleaned out. They had the checks already printed up. We handed over keys and they handed us the checks on the spot. Between the two cars we made a little over 3K in profit. Not bad. It was easier to do than I thought. Kind of a relief. This money will go directly to the overages we're incurring on the home improvements. Our sales guy gives us a lift to the airport in Sean's (old) car. We hop out and head to Enterprise rental car to pick up our new rides. I got a Kia SUV and Sean got a Rav4. We'll have them for the final preparations and then drive them right back to the airport when we leave for Albania. No more car payments. We were spending $1420 a month on those things. Plus, there's car insurance, maintenance, parking meters, gas, and AAA memberships. A lot of money. Because we could. Seems outrageous now that I think about it. Riding around in a rental car makes me feel like we're becoming guests in our own home town. Temporary. With the cars sold, a roommate found for Joan, the new deck railings being stained, and the basement nearing its completion we are proud of our progress. We decide to get away for a bit and head to Washington for some R&R and a continuation of our farewell tour. Catching the sun setting on the Puget Sound was picturesque as always. And without even knowing I was holding my breath I exhaled in a BIG way.

* Day 21 *

A day on the water, hanging with a bunch of guys, and drinking beer on a boat. Attitude adjusted. Laughed so hard. I love being the only girl sometimes. I try not to question how comfortable I am in that particular social setting vs. a group of women. It just is. Well, it's only when they don't treat me like they treat other women. They are still men, but I don't put up with their shit and they know it. I'm just one of them. Equal. Heard. A part of the conversation and banter.

I've always been this way. Haven't taken the time to find my group of women that feed me in the same way. Instead I either avoid social settings or awkwardly stand in the corner with my insecurities. I am the odd man out when it comes to the chit chat of women I find myself around. Most women I've encountered have tough exteriors. Very few are actually relaxed and living in the moment. Too much agenda. Too much multitasking. Too held together. Too much emphasis on appearances.

And I know I can be like that too, but it's amplified while around other women. The feeling of judging tones, awkward body language, and the fake laughter. Sizing up is like a sport and I leave feeling like I'm not enough. That I wore the wrong thing. This is especially worse in a group setting. It could be all in my head, but I don't know how to change it. Growing up looking different than my classmates and navigating the tough complexities of having a bunch of sisters close in age has created an internal struggle that I can't seem to shake. I'm good one-on-one with women who have things in common with my passions and personality. More intimate conversations too. I hate small talk. I'm not good at it. I also dread being one of the little women in the kitchen talking about the pains of motherhood or the latest diet craze while we sip on a spritzer. It's simply not for me. I'm thankful for my guy friends. The way leisure feels natural to them and how that rubs off on me. Guilt free leisure. I can just let me be me. Maybe someday I'll be comfortable enough with who I am to put myself out there and seek girlfriends who work hard and play hard like me. A challenge for another day.

* Day 22 *

Part spontaneity and part I'm not sure when we'll be back, we decide to take in a Mariners game and see Pike Place on our road trip back to Portland. Seattle is a home away from home for me. Many work trips were spent here. Four Seasons on Union Street knew me by name. Shedding a day of exceeding expectations meant running up and down Alaskan Way, then sipping whiskey while staring at the water and the bordering Olympic Mountain range. I'd fantasize about being on the ferries going out to Bainbridge Island. The buzz from the whiskey led me to wonder what it would be like to live here with my family. Like my co-workers do. The price of living is outrageous, but I'd see them more. Then I'd spiral into the impossible art of succeeding in this career and raising a family. How providing for my kids has many meanings. A few years back, I even lived three out of the five work days in a condo, near Amazon headquarters. Straddling two different worlds kept me from fitting fully into either. Time in that zero bedroom studio condo, while being a guest in my own home in Portland, was the loneliest year of my life.

We're all hungry for lunch and the seafood at Pike Place is the best. Fresh. Simple ingredients. We eat and see all the traditional stops at the market. The fish throwing is still an attraction. The chowder is delicious. We down a few oysters and inhale perfectly seasoned tuna tartare while sitting outside under the intense sun rays. Bellies and hearts full, we hop back in the car and head to Safeco Field. All the sights, sounds, and smells of an all American ballgame culminate with the Mariners winning at home. Peanut shells on the ground and cotton candy on the kids' faces make us happy we added this stop to the list.

As we work our way south, Sean has one more thing to cap off this day of nostalgia. We turn off I-5 and head to the ever-famous Frisko Freeze for burgers, fish sandwiches, fries, and milkshakes. This is a place Sean's parents used to go to when they were kids. They grew up around here. Every time we drive to Seattle, Sean talks about stopping here and in 21 years together we finally do. It's like going back in time. The grease seeps through the wax paper bag, but it's damn good. Also, those milkshakes? Best I've ever had. What a trip.

We finally arrive at home and get the kids settled in bed. As I enter Izzy's room to sing her songs, I find her crying under her blankets. She is going to miss her grandma, grandpa, aunties, uncles, and her friends since birth. She lists them all out to me with her hair matted to her face from the tears. At 7 years old, it's too much for her to understand how she'll be without them. Heck, it's too much for me, but I try to hold it together. Her sweet face and quivering lip. I can't take it. I'm doing everything I can to arrange playdates or sleepovers and keep the days upbeat even though I'm losing my shit with all the "stuff." I'm running out of things to say so instead I sing her a bunch of songs after scooping her up and rocking her close to my body like a baby. Thankfully she falls asleep.

* Day 23 *

After five weeks of work on the basement, the painting starts today. It always amazes me, the difference made with a change of color on the walls. A fresh coat, clean lines in the cut work, and the room has been transformed. It feels lighter. Brighter. Bigger. Modern. It's no longer a basement. We will now refer to it as the lower level apartment.

This is really happening. The contractors I hired said they'd try to fulfill my requests, but in the same breath they said it was impossible. Friends, who are contractors, said there was no way I'd even find contractors available this time of year. It's busy season. I love a good challenge and when the word impossible is thrown around it's even sweeter when it all starts falling into place. The bed set I found for the room is going to look beautiful in here. I can't believe I got it for $100. Distressed wood head and footboard sets the vision for the rest of the decor. I can't wait to decorate. I'm going to design it as if it was my own apartment. If it was just me. This is going to be fun.

* Day 24 *

When we first told our parents the news, there was an uneasy but supportive tone to their response. I really didn't know what to expect. When I took my mom to a Mother's Day brunch to let her in on a secret I've been holding for four months, I couldn't even finish my first sentence.

"Mom, I have some news…" Her eyes widened and interrupted. "What? You're pregnant. You're getting a divorce." I shake my head 'no' to both. It's funny how those two things were her knee jerk reactions. Sure, my tone was serious, but nope mom. I'm selling everything off, quitting my job, and moving to Albania. Surprise! Let's drink our mimosas. I told my dad, stepmom, and sisters on a video chat. Shared a phone call and a bunch of texts with my brothers. The thing they all had in common was a total lack of surprise. I mean, they were all surprised the destination was Albania, but leaving to live abroad was something I've talked about since I stopped living internationally 16 years ago. It's like they always knew this was temporary. I hadn't thought of that; the dynamic of my relationships. They knew my heart was somewhere else and now the moment is here.

I thought what would follow would be different, but it really wasn't. We didn't get any more visits than usual. Sure, everyone has their lives, but I thought attendance would go up at the kids' sporting events, maybe a sibling outing or two, or involvement in this big remodel and move. Nothing changed. I was over here and they were over there. The world continued exactly the same.

What does take me by surprise is my parents and Sean's parents, both divorced couples, collaborating on throwing us a goodbye party at our local golf course. An incredibly generous gesture and one I know our family and friends will be happy to attend. The RSVPs have this party close to the size of our wedding. Many of those coming haven't been to Oregon since our wedding 15 years ago. It's like a reunion. They made it kid friendly so Jackson and

Izzy's friends are even coming to the sendoff. Taking place five days before we leave is a little stressful, but family is starting to come to town today. While that happens, Joan continues to move in her boxes. For such a control freak, I'm trying my best to live in a constant state of clutter. Things not in their proper place. I'm trying to relax. To simply enjoy the brunch with my cousin and sister, but the unsettled feeling is making me itch.

* Day 25 *

The house is quiet for the first time in a while. I'm all alone. Sitting at my dining room table for the last time, I start to cry. The last piece of large furniture is sold. The table I always wanted in my home, to have my family sit around and share a meal, is selling for $200. I'm about a week away from moving my entire life to another country. Boxes are everywhere. Walls are bare with spackle drying where we once hung our family pictures. The home doesn't look like mine anymore. I'm driving a rental car. I drop my spoon into my cereal and sob.

6 months ago, we were contacted about the Albania opportunity. A much-deserved promotion for Sean and a direct result of paying for an international recruiting service to shop his education resume around. Admittedly, I didn't have a clue where Albania was when he told me the news so I immediately opened up Google Maps. Europe. Near the bottom of the Italy boot. Right across actually. Bordering the Adriatic Sea. Surrounded by countries I've always wanted to visit. Natural areas practically untouched. A Mediterranean climate with all the changing seasons. Ok, let's do it.

We always thought my global marketing gigs would ship us over, but nothing panned out. With our oldest about to enter middle school, now was the time, and it's happening. Are we crazy? Yes, everyone seems to tell us that, and also that they think we're brave. But we're really not the first people to do this. I have more than a handful of friends who are living or who have lived the expat life. It's them who influenced us. Sharing their stories and seeing them raise their families is an inspiration. We want that life.

For the last 6 years, we've been trying to get a job opportunity to take us to an international address. Actually, we've been trying since we came back from living in Ireland when we were 22. Always having in the back of my mind the way life was there. The life I wanted to get back to. Mental and financial preparation for this moment has been a long journey and now it is happening. I'm a grown adult giddy with excitement. I can feel it in my entire body.

But first, I must do the work. Telling those closest to me and watching their expression shift as I explain we're moving to a place we've never been. Purging, fixing, cleaning, and preparing the current home to become a rental. Interviewing renters and selecting new inhabitants of our family home of 12 years. Selling off anything that held monetary value, donating what we can, and lots of trips to the dump. Spreading our material possessions all over the metro area. All the paperwork and notary visits. Way too many. Canceling all our local subscriptions and contracts. Unplugging. All the checkups and good bill of health sign offs. Giving notice and packing up our desk box to leave our current jobs. Saying goodbye to our family, friends, community, and as many local spots that we can possibly hit before we board the plane. Countless "last time we're going to do this for a while" moments, and a sadness coming over us.

And we are there. At the end of the 6 months of work, the emotional and physical toll is evident. The world has moved fast these past few months and we've pushed ourselves to our limits. Many heavy conversations and tender feelings of loss. Quitting almost happened over and over again. Doubt circled us daily. I don't say this for pity. I am affirming that this decision isn't a light one. I've felt lonely and incredibly loved by my surroundings all at the same time. We have built a wonderful home in the NW and it will be missed.

My path in Albania is unknown. No career move defined for me just yet. I've never lived without this basic structure. It's all new to me. I don't know what will come next, but I am ready. I'm open. To explore, document, learn, love, experience, fail, rebound, and come back.

* Day 26 *

Today is our 15th wedding anniversary. I was asked what we were doing to celebrate and I couldn't help but laugh. Of course, my answer is we're celebrating by moving to Albania. It's the best gift we can give each other. To give our marriage. 15 years is a milestone in any marriage. This month also marks 21 years together. It's hard to believe a whole person can be born and legally drink in the time of our courtship. He was a guy in high school who I detested and I was a girl he couldn't help but keep an eye on and torture with adolescent "I like you" behavior. He signed my senior yearbook, "You suck." If that's not love, I don't know what is. After a camping trip post-graduation, we fell hard and fast. Hot summers in the PNW are the perfect backdrop to a summer romance. During the time I started to figure out who I was, I had him. Bitter and closed off because teenage life had its rough edges, he softened me. Opening up, I shared my dreams of travel. He listened and to my surprise he didn't run away. After college graduation, we applied for a student work visa, whittled everything down to a backpack, said goodbye to everyone that mattered, and hopped on a plane to Dublin, Ireland in fall of 2001. We returned engaged and traveled in fall of 2002. The itch got in our blood early in our relationship. Travel is woven into our DNA. Whenever daily routine seems to be wearing down our connection, we step away. Go somewhere. On the open road, life is breathed back into us. There is an us. It's our home base and every time we come back to it, all is right with the world. Having this in common is what reminds me what great life partners we are to each other. A marriage with a homebody would never work. Exploring and experiencing the world is the basis of the life we've built. We grew up together.

Days before we head on yet another journey after whittling our possessions down, we're sitting in the middle of our local park just six blocks from the house. Familiar smiling neighbor faces all around. The smell of free popcorn popping. Tonight is "Movies in the Park." A summer favorite and definitely a part of our farewell tour. Under the stars, *Kubo and the Two Strings* projects on an inflatable screen. Kids are snuggled under blankets. Adults in lawn chairs drinking wine and beer out of plastic cups. I reach out and hold Sean's hand and whisper, "Happy anniversary babe."

* Day 27 *

The big goodbye party day has arrived. The smell of paint drying in the basement apartment wafts up the stairs as I pour my first cup of coffee. For eleven years, Sean and a bunch of guys have met weekly to golf, drink a few beers, and shoot the shit. Their "me time" to keep their sanity. No women allowed. Of course, he got a lot of eye rolls from me over the years. Spring daylight savings kicks off the Wednesday meet up at Broadmoor and goes until fall daylight savings. So, it's fitting to have part of our sendoff be a scramble tournament at his home course before the party kicks off. There are even trophies to hand out to the winners. I'm supposed to play on Sean and Jackson's team, but I managed to work my way into an appointment with my longtime friend and my one and only hairdresser. Who knows if I'll ever find someone to do my hair in Albania. One of her appointments canceled and now it's my gain. They easily fill my spot in the foursome with our friend, Jenn, who is in town from Boston to attend the party. It's going to be another beautiful summer day in the 90s. I hope they hydrate with more than beer and are in good shape for the party.

I watch the first few teams tee off, hug familiar faces, snap some photos, and then whiz off to Amber's salon. I've known Amber since I was 12 years old. We met in 7th grade homeroom. She was taller than most, dark features, with a big beautiful smile and infectious laugh. I wanted to be her friend as soon as she reached out her hand to shake mine. Luckily, she wanted the same. I nicknamed her long legged piggy one and she promptly responded with calling me short legged piggy one. We got each other. Two independent half Asian girls with estranged dads and everything to prove. She went to beauty school at 19 years old. By 36 she acquired 50% ownership in her own salon and could expand her love for being both a stylist and an educator. Gifted with both the right and left brain strengths, she's become a powerful force in her industry. Needless to say, I have the best. Isn't the saying, "Friends come and go, but a hairstylist is forever"? Lucky for me, I have both.

With Amber being a master colorist, I typically take full advantage and enjoy blues, purples, pinks, reds, or greens woven in somehow. This time I want to pick something that is a change, but easier to maintain. Little did I know that it would be a 5-hour process to change my hair color from a dark brown, almost black, to something more mellow and a softer brown. She dives in anyway. It also gives us time to catch up. With both of us constantly on the go, our moments together seem to happen mostly when she's behind the chair with my hair in her hands. I told her months ago that I was leaving, but I don't think it really hit until now. I can hear it in her tone. Besides being bubbly and funny, she doesn't show other shades of emotions too much. Her sadness is there. I know her. The conversation makes me both happy and sad.

As the party is starting, I leave the salon with a new do that needs another hour to process, but that will have to wait. The parents are going to kill me. I still need to get home and throw on my dress. Ten minutes later I arrive at my house and find Stan staining my front steps. Wanting to chat and ooh and aah over how good they look, I jet past him with a quick hello, wave, and "wow, they look great!" Like Clark Kent, I'm back out the door in minutes running in heels.

I arrive about 45 minutes late. Just before I open the door to the banquet room, I get nervous. Why am I so nervous? I pause and even think about finding a back entrance to sneak in to make a less obvious appearance. Too late. My mom sees me. She's holding her new camera and waving me in. Wait. She never takes pictures. That's always my job in the family.

I hate being the center of attention, but this is my party. There's no escaping it. And there I am. Five steps into the door and my life is flashing before my eyes in the form of many of the people I love. Hugged, kissed, squeezed, smiled at, complemented. About 30 seconds per person. Many of them with the same head tilt as I repeat to everyone how NOT ready I am for the big move. Friend after friend rotates through while my mom acts like the paparazzi.

The whole thing is bizarre. All this, for me? Well for me, Sean and the kids. It's reminiscent of a funeral, wedding reception, and reunion all rolled into one. There are easily 100+ people here. Extended family from all sides of

Sean's and my family. All but one of my siblings. My mom, dad and step mom. Co-workers from my first and my last job. Friends from all our pockets of relationships including a few from elementary school days. A wide assortment of people I just saw last week and some that I haven't seen in years.

Probably inappropriate, but I lean over and tell my mom that I feel like a young man entering at his first strip club. I don't know where to look. Quickly, I apologize. I say stupid things when I'm nervous. In all honesty, I couldn't dream up a better gathering. Looking out, I see my legacy. And I'm too young to have a legacy. Most only get to "see" this floating above a church. Adrenaline suddenly hits me like a ton of bricks. All these faces. All these faces I'm leaving. Oh my gosh, I'm leaving. What am I doing? How can I leave? They are all wishing me well, but I don't feel well. Nauseated I find the nearest bathroom. I place both hands on the cold sink countertop and stare at myself in the mirror. Self soothe. Lots of deep breaths, I start to steady my heart rate. Time for a pep talk. I find talking out loud to myself helps me in times like these. As long as no one is around to hear it. I check the stalls. No feet.

"Relax Amanda. This is what you've been working towards. What you have always wanted. And out those doors are all your family and friends rooting you on. Head to the bar and raise a glass. You fucking deserve all of this. Enjoy this moment."

I always feel stronger when I say the F word. Empowering. That, and whiskey. So that's what I order when I see my brother-in-law at the bar and he asks me what I want. We cheers and the next two hours I do the rounds greeting everyone who made it. I have never felt so lucky. What a web we have woven. In the distance, the kids are playing with their friends. All around me is laughter. Joy. A sense of belonging as all our worlds collide into this huge melting pot. People meeting for the first time, but the common thread of experiences with me or Sean facilitates an easy connection. It is a moment I won't forget and the best gift our parents could give us.

My mom has relinquished the camera duties to my cousin. I approach her and arms are thrown around me in seconds. We sorta sway there. Start to dance and shuffle our feet. She kisses me and tells me she's proud. That she will miss me and the kids, but knows this will bring her daughter happiness.

And that she loves me. I squeeze harder. We pull away and wipe each other's tears. I tell her, "I love you too Mom. And thank you. Thank you for everything." It felt good to sit in her arms for a moment.

I notice there are less people inside and stare out the window to find the driving range in full effect. I run downstairs and see Jackson and his friend Paul going head-to-head in distance drives. Jackson is using his Grandma Joan's driver and consistently hitting between 175 and 200 yards. I challenge him in a mom and son contest. He laughs as he tees me up and I step up with heels and a dress on, ready to swing. The crowd of friends on the balcony cheer me on. To everyone's surprise, even to my own, I smash the ball 250 yards. Jackson makes me do it again to prove it wasn't a fluke. Tees me up and I reach the 220-yard sign. His dimple and disbelief is golden. A nice way to end an incredible night.

* Day 28 *

The fog of last night is still behind my eyes, but there is no time to sleep it off. Time to decorate the lower level apartment with my mom. Sean is so inspired with how the basement turned out that he decides to take on a project of his own. Enlisting the help of our friend Jenn, he gets to work on creating a courtyard entrance to the Airbnb. This is completely his idea and I've never seen Sean motivated to do yard work or a home makeover. I don't know who this is, but I didn't want to stop a good thing. I give him encouraging words and head to the store.

My mom is in her element, but she knows this is my vision. She has an incredible eye for design and doing it in an affordable way. We sift through Home Goods and one find leads to another. We're creating a design palette. We bounce to Best Buy, Home Depot, and Target to find a few more things. It's all starting to come together. This is the first time my mom and I have been alone together since I told her I was leaving. The thrill of our finds mask the other emotions hanging between us. We skirt the topic of Albania a few times, but mostly stay focused on the task for the day. I wanted to talk more, to share what's going on in my head, but it's hard to chat about such a life change when you're comparing mini fridge prices and picking out drapes. Regardless, it just feels good to be with my mom. Her energy at this stage is incredibly helpful because I don't have much left.

Like deranged women we skip lunch and head back to the house to see our vision unfold in the room with our purchases. When we arrive, my cousins and siblings are at the house. I forgot I invited them over before they fly out. There is still a ton to do and the house is a cluttered mess. My family is in the living room sitting on neon colored lawn chairs posing as furniture and all I want to do is hang out. There's just no time. I'm shaking from low blood sugar, but can't stop smiling at the progress of the courtyard designed by Sean and Jenn. He then tells me he snuck in a bowl of pho and that makes me jealous he didn't bring me any. I head downstairs to give my family a tour of the remodel and work with my mom to assemble the bed and hang the decor. I notice her eyes and she slips away to grab her purse. Stress and no eating leads to headaches. Bad ones. Although my mom had plans to hang with the kids tonight, it doesn't look good. She pushed herself too much. I suggest that we all go get a late lunch together, but it's too late for her. With her vision blurred and tracers starting, my brother Ryan offers to drive her home. We'll postpone the kid visit to Sunday night.

We say goodbye to mom and Ryan and I take the rest of my family to a local food cart pod down the street. Sean and I are regulars here with the kids. They can run around, play games, and everyone gets to pick what they want to eat and drink. It's still hot out, but we find some shade. My nephew is playing with a monster truck happy as can be and my niece is napping in her stroller. My brothers-in-law are keeping the day drinking going, while their wives are obviously annoyed. The kids run into their friends. Jackson is playing video games with Paul. And Izzy is pretending to cook in the plastic kitchen with Amelia. As I wait for my food, I'm welling up with tears once again. I step away and sit by myself for a second. Sean and Jenn notice and I wave at them to ignore me.

This is it. The last of it. Actually, I don't think I'll see Ryan again before I fly out. I didn't get the chance to say goodbye. Wednesday is obviously in the middle of the work week. I don't know who can come say goodbye at the airport. I want to hold onto this moment longer, but it's not possible. For something that has felt like a long process, how can it now feel so sudden? My sisters sit by me and I wipe my tears. They start to get sad too. I'm hugging them and I can't pull myself together. They pull away and tell me this isn't the last time I'll see them. I am relieved. We say goodbye, but it's a see you later.

Sean hangs back with the kids. They want to play longer with their friends. I want to sit and do nothing, but Jenn is in town for vacation and spent the whole day doing back-breaking labor on my home with Sean. Dinner and drinks. I at least owe her that and we haven't had a chance to hang out one-on-one yet. I shower, but not much else is spent on my appearance.

I take her to a local spot three blocks from our house. I met this girl on a train in Spain in 2002 and here she is sitting in front of me. We both talk about painful and joyful bits of our lives that have transpired since we first met. How we're both feeling like this is a transition year. She is looking for change and so am I. The difference is my life change is defined right now. Her's is in flux. Our conversation puts both of our minds at ease and I feel even more connected to her. Seeing yourself in someone else gives you a sense of belonging. When I am with Jenn, I don't feel like an outsider. I know there are probably more of us out there, but she's all I need at this moment. The sadness in my heart subsides. I am braver and reassured. Let's go to fucking Albania.

* Day 29 *

I sit straight up in my bed as if I'm catching my breath. The house is still sleeping, but I head downstairs. I continue where my mom and I left off. She's coming over later, but I'm motivated to get done as much as I can. The more efficient we are with this day, the more daylight time she spends with the kids. She is feeling better and we make sure to eat lunch this time. It's all coming together. Proud of what we've accomplished in such a small amount of time, she drives away with the kids for a sleepover.

We have Jenn for a few more hours, before she boards a plane back to Boston, so we head to our favorite taco and margarita shop. She works in operations for a Mexican restaurant. When it comes to work research, Sean and I are always willing participants. Drinks, chips and guac, tacos, and great company. We're feeling celebratory with our friend. Too bad she has to go. As she's checking her flight status, we get a text from our neighbors. They're offering to dig deep in their cellar, aka the basement laundry area, and open a good bottle of wine. Jenn hops in a Lyft to the airport and we head back home to keep the celebration spirit rolling.

Our neighbors Kirsten and John and their kids Sam (7) and Atalay (4) are like family. And when their kids smile, there is nothing much better. It's contagious. We've been neighbors since we moved in. That's over a decade. We walk into their house and I get a big hug from Atalay. Heading in, I realize this is another moment on the goodbye tour. I know we will be back to visit and I can't imagine us not staying lifelong friends, but I don't foresee us coming back to our house to live. For years our kids played together, while we ate, drank, and laughed in each other's backyards. We'd switch off hosting. Our relationship and sense of community defined our kids' childhood up until now. We couldn't have asked for better people to share lives with, and I'm going to miss them.

Kirsten grabs me a glass after we select a bottle and head outside. The quiet and calm is nice. Another warm evening in the NW. Barefoot around their wrought iron table in the grass, we talk into the night. I am thankful for the unplanned visit and the eyes and smiles of my friend. Her companionship puts me at peace.

* Day 30 *

Two more days. Contractors are back to perform last little bits to the lower level apartment bathroom to call it complete. It's totally random, but we were able to snag an old co-worker's queen bed mattress after I saw her advertise it on Facebook. Talk about last minute, but the bed with all the bedding looks great. I can't believe I did it. There wasn't an ounce of room for error. A sliding barn door to the bedroom will be installed after we've left, but everything else is complete. Standing in the bedroom, my bare feet love the squish and comfort of the new carpet. I stretch my arms out and twirl around like Julie Andrews in *The Sound of Music*. I'm proud of myself.

I fill my rental car with a few returns and I message my old co-worker Kim. The stores are right next to the office of my most recent job. She said she had a gift for me and I wanted to say goodbye again anyhow. I'm standing in the middle of Home Goods when I see an even older co-worker. He's looking at bed sheets and we recognize each other. He was a writer I worked with a couple of agencies ago. We have the typical small talk. I tell him I'm working on decorating my Airbnb and then casually drop that I'm leaving for Albania on Wednesday. His expression is classic, but my tone is different than the other times I've shared the news. It has more confidence. There isn't an inflection at the end of Albania. Without question, we are doing this. He wishes me luck and we part ways as I see my friend Kim approaching me with a great big smile.

Kim has been my ray of sunshine the last two years. Leaving a 14 year advertising agency career to become the director of marketing for a small tech startup wasn't easy. There were a lot of firsts for me. I was the entire marketing department. Kim was also a team of one heading up her department of client service. We commiserated quite a bit and her positive influence kept me going even when I was running on fumes. She thoughtfully arranged my company send off and now here she is with a gift bag and more hugs.

Before my last day at the company, she and two other co-workers golfed with me at Broadmoor. It was a great day of 18 holes and riding in the golf cart with her by my side. In the middle of the store, she pulls out a necklace she had made, with the latitude and longitude coordinates of the golf course. Using latitude and longitude was common in our work together, so the detail is even more touching. Now we're hugging and crying. The whole scene is pretty funny. I'm a big believer that each of my work paths were designed to introduce certain people to me. She and I were meant to meet. I will miss her.

With most of the odds and ends complete, I head to my last dance class at BodyVox for a while. Mondays at 6pm have been my time to re-acquaint myself with my passion for dance. My moment of balance, breath, and release. It's my church. I found Tracey Durbin in the first neighborhood I owned a home. Walking past the dance studio, while on a date with Sean, my eyes filled with wonder again. I hadn't danced for a while. Just stopped. Finding adult dance classes are a challenge. Especially if you aren't a beginner. The whole industry doesn't cater to people that grew up dancing. We simply age out. But not with Tracey and the Luigi (Louis Facciuto) inspired format she teaches. When she left the studio and moved across the country last year, I couldn't help but reflect on the impact she made on me and others. I wrote.

> *Patterns and routines.*
> *Familiar faces and feet planted we move together in meditation.*
> *Young. Old. Experienced. New.*
> *The body takes over and the energy lifts the heart.*
> *Patterns and routines.*
> *Grounded to appear heavy, weighted,*
> *our outstretched arms press through the air.*
> *Our necks elongated.*
> *Spines finding space that make us a few inches taller.*
> *Patterns and routines.*
> *Rooms can be entered, but not many are like this.*
> *It's a place where repetition heals you.*

And I'm not alone. We all need this.
She did this.
Patterns and routines.
Threads from one shared evening to the next.
The moments in between disappear and you pick up where you left off.
Present. Aware. This is special.
She is special.
Patterns and routines.
Contractions wring out the body, the breath that was held in small pockets
An exhale that was never so deep.
The watchful eye will find more here.
I found me.
Patterns and routines.
A visual treat to indulge upon
the unique qualities of every active participant
unfolds on top of the shapes she imagines
We add us.
Patterns and routines.
Where movement is a form of remembering
and taught control stabilizes the spirit.
The integrity of the technique
is ever present in the passion of her delivery.
Patterns and routines.
Quietly connecting, there is a closeness
a dependency on the dance
and our guide in self-expression.
Entrenched in the sincerity of her intention
the void is now loud.
The only way to fill it is to give thanks
and live in gratitude of her patterns and routines.

One of her dancers took the torch and continues to teach her class with choreography collaboration from Tracey. Moving my body, in that room, felt right tonight. As we dancers say, I felt "on." Mind, heart, body, and spirit aligned.

* Day 31 *

Final stretch. I keep trying to get the mental health in check, but I can't deny how tired I am by all this. I wake at 4am again. Many remaining things to check off the list. I know we're close, but not yet there. As if there's not enough to do in the day, I'm meeting Amber at 8am to color correct my hair. It needs to process one more time and then get styled again. Bonus is I'll have great travel hair. The whole thing is pretty quick and my mind is distracted. Alone in the salon, I at least get to say one more goodbye as I rush out the door like a Pantene commercial.

Time to pack. For a girl who loves to travel, I rethink it sometimes simply because I hate packing. And this isn't a typical packing job. I vacuum-pack what's left, make each crate weigh less than 50 pounds, and hope we don't have to leave too much behind. Ugh. Gonna have to dig deep on this. But first, time to meet the other renter of the home. Joan's roommate.

We gather around Joan's dining room table. Ours has long been sold off. Sitting in her chairs, I catch myself looking around. I don't even recognize the house. I know I'm rushing, but I have to get through this to get back to packing. We do a walk-through of the house, exchange keys, answer last minute questions, and let her know that house cleaners will be at the house tomorrow morning after we head to the airport. She can move in any time after 12pm. We shake hands and that's that. I don't have time to process what's really happening here. She doesn't say much either, but I scoot her out the door to get back to sorting what's what and then attach my vacuum to the plastic bag to suck out the air. Must shrink down. Even with all the purging, I have to leave part of my wardrobe behind, but most everything else should fit. Our flight takes off at 2pm, which leaves the morning to finalize everything.

The compressed bags are irregular shapes that don't stack nicely in the crates. I can't get the lids on and I'm pretty sure we're over the maximum weight. I could do more, but I have to stop and get in the shower. Our other neighbors Katie and Justin are throwing us a goodbye BBQ at their house a couple blocks away. They have a gorgeous outdoor backyard space. Our daughters have been friends since birth and we've all been friends about the same amount of time. Neighbor John, an executive chef in his past life, has been slow cooking his cioppino all day. My sisters are coming and other friends as well. It will be another great night at the Transeth's. The kids are anxious and impatient while I get ready. I send them ahead with Sean and my sister Reyna. I'm left alone in our big empty house trying to hold back emotions. Need to avoid my makeup running all over the place before I even get there. Waterproof mascara. Time to apply heavily.

With a new mustard colored dress on, the necklace from Kim adorning my neckline, and the sun shining on my face as I walk over there, I am hopeful. I'm smiling. Yes, we've spent a lot of time and energy on saying goodbye, but not nearly enough thinking about what we are embarking on. This is happening tomorrow. We did it. It was hard, but here we are. All our dedication. Our preparation. My steps slow. My smile starts to fade. We're moving to a place we've never been. There's not even much you can learn about it online. We know no one there. We'll be taking on a whole new lifestyle while completely altering our family dynamic and roles. We're leaving a good life. Good people. We really have no idea what to expect. We could absolutely hate it. It could be the worst mistake of lives. My steps start to quicken. I recall my timely fortune cookie from lunch. The small piece of paper read, "Tomorrow is a good day for trying something new." Damn. I need a drink.

Chapter 4

Adventure isn't a destination. It's a frame of mind.

* Day 32 *

Today is the day. Although my neighbors went above and beyond last night, they insist on doing even more. My friend Laurie also shows up and I give her a tour of the place. She is blown away with everything. Coming back upstairs, I see mimosas, coffee, bagels, yogurt and fruit spread out on our kitchen counter. We're completely and utterly spoiled with kindness. How can we leave these people? Our village.

I've put it off long enough. There are no more days left. We must finalize the packing. With the fresh energy of neighbor Kirsten and her scale, we strategically figure out the puzzle to make this all work. Sean's dad and stepmom have arrived too. Many emotions are raw at this point. I cannot believe everything is packed up. Five crates, six suitcases, and four backpacks all set out on the curb. I walk through the rooms one by one saying my own personal goodbye. Reminiscing about the first time I walked on these hardwoods and put in an offer on the house the same day. I run into Sean doing the same thing. People are calling to us from downstairs, but we both stand there holding each other. His lip is quivering, but his expression reassures me. No matter what happens, I know he and I can overcome anything together. We've built a great life together so far. Why stop now? In my ear, he tells me he loves me while giving me a tighter squeeze. I ask for a moment alone.

Sean is the kind of guy that likes to be at the airport many hours in advance. Me, I like to arrive at the airport and walk on the plane. I can tell Sean is anxious about getting there. I take one last look. This 100+ year old home treated us well. It really is beautiful. Goodbye house.

Shutting the door, I notice everyone waiting by the curb and starting to put the crates in the cars. Wait! I need us with all the luggage in front of our house to capture this moment forever in a photo. I get slumped shoulders as a response because Sean sees the clock ticking, but I know he'll thank me later. Meanwhile, our dog Jazzy is clawing at the front door. Scratching and mad that her family is leaving her behind to live with Joan. My heart. We'll be back to get her at Christmas once we're settled, but it hurts to see her little head through the window in the door. Poor Jazzy girl.

We're only 10 minutes from the airport. It feels even less when we arrive to drop off our rental cars. Sean's dad has all the crates and the kids in his truck. We meet him curbside and wheel everything to check-in. Passports in hand, we watch each piece of luggage make its way on the conveyor belt. With time to spare, we decide to have lunch with Sean's mom, dad, stepmom, and my mom. Last few moments with the grandparents.

The attitude of the kids is upbeat and it keeps everyone else trying to match the mood, but we adults look like gravity is pulling us down. Their opinions on the situation are muted. We know they don't want us to go. They don't understand this and I know we're breaking their hearts. All the nonverbal cues around the table express it. My mom is actually flying to California today for work so she'll be able to come to the gate with us. As we finish eating, the moment to say goodbye to Sean's parents has come. Izzy and Jackson start to get agitated. We walk to the security line and Izzy starts breaking down. Crying and grabbing her Papa Dan. Everyone is in tears, but Izzy is sobbing saying over and over again that she doesn't want to go. She doesn't want to leave. Dan is keeping such a great dialogue with her. He tells her it's ok. He will miss her, but he's so excited for her too. Strangers around us feel for our situation. The scene is awful. Dan, Bonnie, and Joan stand there behind the ropes. Their faces a wreck and our kids listless in our arms. We try our best to comfort, but Bonnie realizes staying there isn't helping. She motions to Dan, and Joan follows. We get one last look and say goodbye over the heads in line with us.

We make it through security and my mom comes with us to our gate. To distract the kids, we grab a few drinks and snacks for the plane, but they know it's time. One more goodbye. The intercom announces our flight and invites family with children to board. The tears are back and we're all embracing my mom. We get to the gate and Izzy breaks away to run back to hug grandma one more time. This is killing me seeing her like this, but we are patient with her and more strangers witness their connection. Heads tilting with compassion, they let me scoop her up without crowding us from holding up the line. I catch my mom's eyes one last time as she waves me on.

Now seated on the plane, I'm able to calm Izzy and even myself. I immediately start composing an email to all our family urging them to download WhatsApp to follow along and get updates from us as we travel. I get it sent off before we leave and even start a group to invite people. I can't lose connection right now. If I can't have them by my side, digital connection will have to do. I need their support to get through this.

The earth under the plane leaves us and we are off. We're leaving our lifelong hometown and all our family and friends, but we are moving towards a promise Sean and I made to ourselves. Living internationally as a family was our dream before we even gave birth to our first child. Sitting in my seat on the plane, I look down the row and see our kids settled in with headphones on, watching a movie, eating the airplane food. Here come my tears, again.

Above 10,000 feet, I hop on the WiFi and communicate in the family WhatsApp group the whole time. Technology is amazing. We land in Chicago, but we had a slight delay and our gate is on the other side of the airport. We consult a security guard and he has his doubts we'll make our flight. There's a shuttle that goes to our gate, but it's a 10-15 walk and the last one leaves in 20 minutes. If we don't make it, we have to go back outside and through security all over again. Before he can even finish telling us which direction, we're running top speed like a scene from *The Breakfast Club*. The kids are keeping up and people are clearing the way. We're feeling good with the time we're making because we're running and not walking. We arrive at the desk and the security guard tells us we just missed it. It left 10 minutes earlier than it was supposed to and we're crushed. Sean's hands are in the air while he's pacing to contain his anger. She doesn't seem to have any sympathy for us. In her monotone way, like she's said it a zillion times, she directs us how to go all the way around through security. We know we need to run again or we're not making the plane. I offer a few words of encouragement, crack a joke about how we're getting our wiggles out before getting on a plane for 10 hours, and off we go.

It's close, but we make it. We're sweating and notice the constrained space of this flight heading to Istanbul, Turkey. Talk about no leg room. Sean is sitting with the kids in the same row and I'm a row ahead in a window seat. As everyone starts piling in, the space feels smaller and smaller. I've flown a lot of international flights and this is the tightest quarters yet. That's alright. I'll make the most of it. I'm moving to Albania. I put in my headphones and pick my first of probably four movies for this long 10-hour flight.

Sadly, the cheesy rom-com isn't enough of a distraction. There is zero air circulation in my area. Maybe it's because I'm wedged against the window by a middle-seat-guy spreading his legs and feet into my space. Or the fact that the man in front of me has his seat leaning back as far as it goes, which means his head is in my lap. I try my best to express my discomfort with both of them, but neither want to admit they can understand me. Sweating, I feel a mini panic attack coming on. Small spaces sometimes do that to me. My phobia goes all the way back to when I was 6 or 7 years old and I got stuck in a hide-a-bed playing with my siblings. I turn around to Sean and give him the eye contact that means business. I can't do it. I wake up middle-seat-guy and push myself through the obstacle of limbs to break free. Trying to catch my breath, I stand in the aisle explaining my situation to Sean and wiping the beads of sweat from my face. My heart racing. I know I am asking a lot, but I need to switch and sit with the kids instead. At least in increments. These guys in the other seats will listen to Sean. I'm sure of it. They couldn't care less about my comfort. Sean's not happy about moving seats, but he gets it too. He puts both men in check with his elbows and knees and then passes out asleep. What a sigh of relief.

Call it strange, but I enjoy watching the flight pattern. Especially when it's a long distance. I pause my movie and switch to see where we are over the ocean. 17 years ago, Sean and I boarded a plane to Ireland, with only our backpacks, and settled in a Galway apartment. Now here I am with our kids on a flight to live internationally again and our flight pattern is taking us right over Galway. It has to be a good sign. We give our friends and our old home a wave from above.

* Day 33 *

Shuffling through the airport for our last flight of the day, we get to our gate. I am a sucker for signs and admit I can place meaning on just about anything. Our gate number happens to be 503, which was our area code in Oregon, and again I feel like this means good things are coming. Like this was all meant to be, and the universe is reassuring us to keep going. Or to turn around and go back?

Time to board. We hop on an outside shuttle to take us all of 50 feet. Sean looks like a giant among the people on the bus. He looks back at me and we both smile at each other thinking the same thing. In the US, he isn't considered a large guy, but when we travel outside of the country a broad shouldered, 6-foot-tall, 250-pound man is out of the ordinary. We take off just as the sun is setting. The sky in pink hues. Izzy leans to look out the window. I grab her hand and squeeze. Final leg. No turning back now.

Arriving is all so surreal. Three plane rides put us in what feels like another universe. The August air is warm, but not too humid. A big pink T-Mobile sign, targeting English speaking tourists (that's us now), is hanging from the ceiling, front and center. Everyone starts to pick a line in front of the border control booths. I feel delirious, but relieved. We are finally here. We did it. Well, now what? I brush off the lost feeling for the moment. I'm having a hard time standing in line to get our passports stamped. Legs are weak and a bit numb. The kids look beat. My phone buzzes and it looks like signing up for Google's Project Fi is working. I have cell service. No thanks, T-Mobile. I have no idea what time it is back at home, but I message the family chat anyway. We have safely landed in Tirana, Albania.

Next challenge is baggage claim. Quickly we realize the five suitcases we checked didn't arrive, but our crates did. With the tight turn in Chicago we had a feeling this would happen. I stay with the crates and the kids while Sean does his best talking with the customer service representatives to locate the suitcases. A security guard tells me no one will bother the bags and encourages me to join Sean. I stay exactly where I am. I'm not that trusting. After about 20 minutes and a few phone calls, we learn that they are stuck in Chicago and will be coming on a later flight. There's nothing more we can do tonight. They give us a number to call in the morning and we walk away hoping it will all work out. What else can we do?

On the upside, the school Director, Sean's boss Alan, is at the airport to greet us as we pass airport security. In a sea of well-dressed dark eyed men and a few women dressed in all black with a white scarf over their head, we easily spot him. White hair and beard, dressed in a white linen shirt. I shake his hand as his smile transports some comfort to this worn out mom. His part British and part Aussie accent is rattling off a bunch of things, but I'm in a daze. As we exit through the sliding doors of the airport, a big plume of cigarette smoke hits us in the face. He arranged for a large van to pick us and our luggage up and even brought a bag of groceries to get us started when we wake in the middle of the night confused about what time zone we're in. What a pleasant surprise and incredibly welcoming. It's dark out and the humid air feels like it is getting heavier as it gets later.

Alan leads us to the taxi driver and we pile our crates in the back while he attempts to speak English to a driver who doesn't speak English. Not wanting to worry us, he tells us the driver has our landlord's number to call if he can't find the home. It already feels like an adventure. I have wandered aimlessly with Sean in many foreign countries, but this time we have two kids to worry about and must avoid alarming them at all costs. Alan assures us it's a quick drive from the airport to our new place. He then waves goodbye as we pull away. Just the Maileys and an Albanian stranger. Let's go.

With our luggage taking up most of the room in the van, I squeeze on the bench up front in between the driver and Sean. Very cozy. Had our other bags arrived, I'm not sure where we would have put them. The ice is broken as I hear Drake's "*God's Plan*" playing on the radio. I look at Sean and listen to the taxi driver shifting through the gears. With each gesture of his arm, I realize he doesn't have enough room unless I lift up my butt. Not awkward at all. Izzy is staring out the window and Jackson is asleep. The driver says nothing until he's yelling on the phone in Albanian. I am assuming he's talking to our landlord.

All of a sudden the van stops. We pull up to a gate. It's really dark in what seems to be a small side street. Now nearly 10 pm local time (1 am PT), I see an older man and woman, as well as a man in his 20s who appears to be their son. The woman grabs Izzy's head in her hands and kisses her on the forehead. She introduces herself as Violto. Our landlords give us a warm welcome in their late evening. Incredibly generous. They help get our crates up a flight of stairs into our apartment. Their son, Claudio, speaks English but Violto's eyes lead me around as she opens up the windows in each of the rooms to let the air in. The place is much bigger than I thought. The pictures sent from the previous owner didn't do it justice. Claudio turns on the air conditioner, tells us the WiFi password, connects with Sean on WhatsApp, and leaves us for now.

After 26 hours of travel door-to-door to our new home we are spent. We hit the bed fast.

Chapter 5

Embrace moments that reveal why you must dream bigger.

* Day 34 *

It's Friday. 5am local time. I can't sleep anymore. Laying on this rock hard bed, I am wide awake. Jet lag is in full effect, but that means I'm up in time to watch the sunrise. Even with groggy eyes, I now fully see and take in this beautiful apartment we've landed. Three bedrooms, two bathrooms, with four balconies, a laundry room and modern kitchen. The kitchen and laundry room are a huge surprise. When we lived in Ireland, we didn't have a large refrigerator or oven and the washer/dryer combo appliance was in the kitchen. Albania being the second poorest country in Europe, I was preparing myself for something even less accommodating. The layout is perfect for our family of four. It even feels like more space than our previous home because everything is on one level. It's furnished with items I wouldn't choose, but who cares. It's not a hotel room. We lucked out stepping off the plane and into our new home. No searching. I feel spoiled. How can this be only 700 euros a month?

Hearing my stomach growl, I dig into the groceries from Alan. Instant coffee and toast with butter and strawberry jam. Thankful for the simple things because I can figure out the kettle and toaster, but the stove and microwave aren't so easy. The symbols are like a riddle I can't make any sense of with such little sleep. A task for another time.

I sip down three cups of coffee on the balcony off the kitchen as the sky changes with the sun rising over the Dajti mountains. What a cliff face. I set up the table and two chairs that were folded in the corner. My skin feels tight and swollen from the travel, but watching an old woman walk up and down our street with a wheelbarrow full of what appears to be corn has me smiling from ear to ear.

I grab my computer to check in on the world back at home. Technology is truly amazing. We're doing our banking online and through mobile apps. Our Spotify account still works here so I'm streaming music as I recount the last few days. Email. Google Fi. WhatsApp. Social Media. Airbnb. Netflix. Chromebooks. Google Translate. Google Maps. PayPal. All of it. None of this existed when Sean and I lived in Ireland in 2001. What a different world we live in.

Sean joins me on the balcony. He poured himself a cup of instant coffee too and we sit in quiet for a minute. The kids still in bed. Warm air on our face. We both observe the steady foot traffic going up the street. The crow of the roosters. The chirp of the small birds on the wires strung and exposed from the poles. The wandering of what seems to be two stray dogs. The unfinished buildings that surround us. The marked one way road that people seem to be using as a two way. The luscious fruit and olive trees in the garden area of our gated villa. It's all a lot to take in. Our eyes wide and expressions still in shock of what we just did.

Sean gets a message from Claudio. He offers to take Sean in his car to buy a TV and get groceries to get us started. The generosity continues. In the meantime, I'll wait for the kids to get up, make them breakfast, and start to unpack. Teamwork.

Izzy's carrying her blanket and finds me on the balcony. She's hungry and doesn't know what day it is. Her cute traveled face looks up at me and smiles. I get her set up to watch her cartoons on her Chromebook and Jackson wakes up next. I crack the symbol code on the stove and manage to make scrambled eggs and toast. A moment of proud mom mojo. Like because I figured that out, I can now make anything work out in this new country. Riiight.

Bellies full and jet lag is lagging. Let's unpack to keep busy. Although we're pulling old things out of our crates, they somehow feel new. We start to set up the kids' rooms and I learn they don't know how to put clothes on a hanger, fold their clothes, or ball up their socks. I feel like a failed mom for a minute.

The support of their grandmas, me, and even house cleaners have spoiled them. They aren't learning self-sustaining life skills. This is going to change.

In all the unpacking, we find the travel kits Grandma Joan packed in the kids' backpacks. Our toiletries are in the suitcases that didn't come and I'm excited for yet another win this morning. Teeth brushing can be magical. I can see the kids start to lose steam. Izzy almost fell asleep in the pile of clothes on her floor. Sean isn't back yet, but I comply and help them into their beds for a nap. No need to force them on the time zone too hard just yet. They look so peaceful sleeping. I want to join them, but I know how the jetlag game goes. We're nine hours ahead. It's going to take close to nine days to feel normal. I need to try to stay up to shave that down to six or seven days.

Sean arrives and he's buzzing. They haul in all the groceries and he rattles off all the things he saw. It was so dark last night. I haven't seen anything in our new neighborhood yet and I'm jealous as he fills me in. He was able to score a new smart TV that includes Netflix. We hurry to get it all assembled and hooked up to Jackson's Xbox before the kids wake from their nap. We say our goodbyes and thank Claudio. We have about an hour of quiet time together. Wide eyed we keep staring at each other. What we did is starting to set in. We're living in Albania.

The kids wake up like it's Christmas morning. None of us knew what to expect here. We thought many of these luxuries would be things we'd have to say goodbye to. As a mom, I'm wary of device dependency, but at the same time, they're comforting because they're amenities they associate with home. I let it go.

Before the sun goes down, we get out and walk around the neighborhood a bit. Get our bearings. We stumble upon a nearby mall, a few restaurants, and even a dance studio. My first impression is surprise. Tirana is much more developed than I thought it would be. Unfortunately, our bags still haven't arrived, but unpacking what we had in the crates is making this apartment already feel homey.

* Day 35 *

Izzy wakes up crying. I pull her into our bed and snuggle her. She holds on tight. I'm barely awake, but my heart is sad that she is sad. She misses her grandparents a lot. On repeat all day every day, "I miss grandma. I miss papa." Even though I could sleep for another few hours, I pull myself out of bed to arrange a video call with family. The time zone allows us to talk to them at the end and the start of their day. I think this works well for us. As soon as she sees their faces and hears their voices, she lights up. I hope the dependency subsides. Nonetheless, it helps start the day on the right foot.

Doing the sink full of dirty dishes, I am disappointed there is no dishwasher. Then I open up my blinds. As I wash slowly, people are walking up and down our street to start their day. Some carrying garbage to drop in the three dumpsters at the top of the street. Some carrying groceries and jugs of water. Others are simply commuting by foot. To my left, I see a wheelbarrow flying up in the air on a pulley system across the street. Two men are setting a roof on a large pink building. Wet cement comes up in the wheelbarrow which is loaded by the guy down below. The man on the roof pulls it up, shovels it out and sends it back down empty. He then proceeds to use a trowel to spread the cement out and lay the clay tiles while the man below uses his shovel to break out the remnants of the older cement, so it doesn't set, and then shovels in more wet cement to send back up. Sean joins me, grabs a towel, and starts to dry the dishes. We watch together. He leans in and says, "This street is something we will always remember." I can feel my face smile. I could get used to this. What dishwasher?

To beat the jet lag, we venture out to sightsee in our new home city. The town is alive. My eyes fill with colorful sights. The rubble of older buildings and the modern post communism development is similar to the "progress" we witnessed in Vietnam. It's beautiful to see past and present architecture together instead of wiped out like we saw in places like Germany that had no trace of the past buildings. It brings an increased meaning all around. Add to that, seeing my family walking these streets in front of me and the whole scene is bizarre.

We move on to visit Bunk'art 2. Repurposing a real bunker, the art installation reconstructs the history of the Albanian Ministry of Internal Affairs from 1912 to 1991 and reveals the secrets of "Sigurimi", the political police used as a harsh persecution weapon by the regime of Enver Hoxha. Bunk'art 2 is the first major video museum exhibition dedicated to the victims in Albania during the communist era.

Our eyes can't even blink. We learn of the fall of communism in 1991 and the price paid by many trying to leave their country to escape Hoxha's dictatorship. A crime punishable by death. For nearly 50 years, no one was allowed to come in or go out. Roads and freeways weren't developed in an effort to restrict planes and helicopters from landing. Only Hoxha could travel on the one lane road and very few were even granted a driver's license.

The juxtaposition of people back at home, floored that we would even want to embark on this journey, is interesting. This country was secluded. Its citizens were forced to stay in country. Many back at home choose to never leave the US or even their own state. Trump's power and influence is being referenced as a dictatorship. Standing in this bunker, learning of Albania's protest to fight for their freedom to roam the world and not be held in a policed state, is moving. Chilling.

The day ends with Jackson telling me, "I think I'm starting to feel like this can be home." We all sleep heavy that night.

* Day 36 *

Having slept through most of the night, I feel new. I was in bed by 12:30am local time, but slept 'till 7:30 am. We're taking it nice and slow this morning, but soon we'll set out to meet the mountains.

Jumping into a taxi, with broken English and Albanian on Google translate, we make our way to Dajti Ekspres. About 15 minutes from City Center, we embark on the longest cableway in the Balkans. The Austrian built cable car dangles over lush trees that look like broccoli, milky blue green water reservoirs, and roaming pastures with goats, chickens, horses, and cows. Sprinkled throughout you can spot a few of Hoxha's cement bunkers tucked in the rock. As you climb over 5,000 feet to the top, the valley opens up and looking in the opposite direction you can see full city views of Tirana as you get closer and closer to the rocky terrain. Just as we get to the complex at the top of Dajti, my fear of heights kicks in as the cable car dips too close to the cliff edge in my opinion. It feels like we are going to hit the side of the mountain at any moment. Thankfully, we arrive safely and walk out to an incredible National Park with plenty of green space to stretch out and feel the cooler temperatures on our skin. Before we explore, we stop in at a beautiful restaurant, Ballkoni Dajtit, that sits on the edge of the cliffside. The wood exterior and log cabin architecture blends nicely with the natural setting. Like a tree house perched. The entire back of the restaurant is lined with floor to ceiling windows that face Tirana. Window slabs stagger and have 2-feet spaces in between to enjoy the scenery and fresh air. The novelty of the open glass is nice, but we all giggle about how this would never fly in the US. Someone is bound to fall.

Enjoying a glass of wine, I remember we're sorta on vacation in the beginning. This life can't possibly continue at this pace both in excursions and spending. Normalcy will start to settle in as Sean and the kids head to school, but I am happy to make great use of the time before all that starts, and try on a different pace for the family. End the American addiction to convenience so we can do more in a day. A hovering feeling and steady heartbeat of "just keep working" so you can "keep buying" and give your kids "more than you had." Do more together vs. simply being spectators to our children's lives. Try enough new, but hold onto a few traditions and routines.

Today, I am opting to participate with the kids. Fueled up with Albanian dishes, we walk the grounds. Horseback riding, bb gun shooting, playground structures, bouncy castle, it has it all. We make our way to the Adventure Park. Alongside their little bodies, I'm moving through a ropes course for the first time. The height of the course is a bit unnerving and I can feel every muscle in my body. In fact, I'm shaking. It's incredibly challenging, but thrilling at the same time. I love the way Jackson looks at me while we conquer all five courses together. Each one ends with an even higher and longer zipline. Another first for me. He coaches me the whole time. Like he is proud of me and enjoys being a motivator for his ol' mom. I notice other mothers standing below taking pictures of their kids. That is typically me, but here I am. The air feels nice and I could stay in the trees forever. Jackson decides to go through again, but I sit it out to rest, watch the sun peek through the trees, and let my mind wander.

I think too many of "more of the same" or life routines on repeat gives the impression that time is suspended. A falsity that can suck you under because it's comfortable. I think it's where the phrase "where does the time go" comes from. I want to feel the time lived. Take pride in caring for our home with our own hands and energy. Understand distance by walking it on foot. Celebrate a modest living surrounded by just enough. Revel in the discovery that we are more than our occupations, our stations. That there are many ways to fill a day. Listen to the lessons of others and respect all ways of living. Put energy into entertainment that is outward, experiential. Seek to be a positive influence, while not being naive about the pains of the world. Live in a state of hopefulness by noticing those moments that perpetuate joy. Some would argue that I could do all these things at home. I sure tried. The constant glamour of "busy" and the "hustle" was simply too attractive for me. I know that breaking away was necessary in all this. We were truly seduced by the chasing of the American Dream.

The sun is hanging low in the sky so we grab a taxi to head back into town. Our driver is blasting 2Pac as a nod to us being American. He happens to pick the song most loaded with curse words. "*Hit em Up*" is bumping while we drive down the mountain and the kids are giving me eyes. All we can do is bust up laughing.

We get home and we're starved. Another day ending with a struggle to find a restaurant for dinner. There are bars and cafes everywhere, but there is no food. Just a place to drink espresso for hours, smoke cigarettes, and eat ice cream. We even went in the mall because we saw a sign reading, "food zone." Nope. Nothing edible there. Sean and I start laughing truly wondering if people eat at all. Maybe that's why everyone is so skinny. Coffee and cigarettes. Rinse repeat. Tired from the adventure park we feel a bit defeated. We head into the grocery store for the first time and amazingly find many of our familiar American brands. Tonight, we're making pasta, salad, and garlic bread. It doesn't need to be all new all the time. Comforts of home sprinkled in is calming.

* Day 37 *

Changing life direction and residency like this isn't conventional. Friends and family back at home keep asking me if I feel safe. "Does it feel hostile?" "Are people nice?" My reply wants to be, "I felt less safe in the US than I do here," but that wouldn't be patriotic of me I suppose. But it's true. My heart and mind is at ease and it's not just because I'm not working. The current toxic nature of American culture is making people sick. Depressed. Codependent. Less adventurous. Paranoid. Fearful. Held down by the heavy state of affairs. School shootings and emboldened bigotry. Growing homelessness. The disappearance of the middle class. Someone like Trump being elected into office. Those with a strong mental health can overcome, but it takes a focused discipline that becomes all consuming. This life is all new, but I already feel like I can breathe again.

We are not denying our citizenship or our love of the community we have back at home. In fact, the good parts are even more pronounced 6,002 miles from home. There are components of our American lifestyle and community that you can see integrated in our life, but I know there is more out there to be discovered, incorporated, reflected upon. Exposure, absolute exposure, is the goal. My aperture is open and just like when I was a child I am still an insatiable sponge. Curious. If I'm not in a state of learning and seeing more, I collapse inward.

As I'm in the fog of writing, I get a phone call from my mom and mother-in-law. I am now a property manager and these two are my wonderful helpers. Of course, I couldn't just leave the house, have renters move in, and not expect there to be things to address. That would be too easy. I get an earful followed up by an "official complaint email" from my renter living in Izzy's old bedroom. A challenge to navigate, but I'm sure it will resolve as it's meant to. Time to put my communication, project management, and team leadership skills to work.

Just before lunch time, we meet up with Joe, the Vice Principal of the primary school and Sean's designated "buddy." He lives not far from us and offered to tour us around to point out his go to spots, answer questions, and even take us by the school. Soft spoken and overall quiet demeanor, Joe leads and we follow. Sean is walking the closest to him. He has a hard time hearing anyone. Even loud me. I can barely hear too, but we end up stopping for pizza. Listening to him, it's nice to get a local expat perspective and talk with someone that's been in the international program for years. Puts us at ease. After lunch, we head to the school. I can't believe how close it is to our house. About a 6-7 min leisurely walk. Jackpot.

The school building was built by the communist party and used to train college kids in communist beliefs and propaganda. The outside structure definitely feels of that time, but when the front doors open and the lobby is revealed it feels much softer. Beautifully redesigned space. I take Sean's hand. He looks excited and he should be. A huge upgrade from what we left in Oregon. I'm proud of all he has done with his life and career. This moment has the weight of something defining. I go on the best adventures with this man by my side.

* Day 38 *

I arranged for a tour guide to take us to Durrës in his car. Sean learned from Joe that there is a bus that can take us there for less than a dollar each, but the process doesn't sound appealing. In Joe's words,

> "You go to the bus stop near the school. You'll see a man yelling 'Durrës Durrës' over and over again. You go to him and tell him you want to go to Durrës and pay him 70 lek. He will then guide you to a bus that is waiting to be filled up. There is no time table. The bus goes when it's full. Highly recommend you go around 7am. Once you're on the bus, don't worry if it stops. It's common for the driver to park the bus and get out to have a coffee or snack while in route. The trip should take around 30-60 min to get there. 20-30 min if you drive yourself. Once you're there, you'll need to keep an eye out for the bus. Again, it won't leave until it is full. They go every hour or even sooner in the summer hours. Good luck and let me know how it goes."

Of course, that process didn't sit well with either of us newbies in a country we know nothing about and don't speak the language. I've been here for five days and haven't seen the beach yet. The gorgeous beaches are all that's online when you search for information about Albania. That and communism. To feel more comfortable, we pay the high price for a guide to get us there and to teach us more about Albania. We meet him at the school to avoid disclosing where we live. Again, it's a trust thing. Sean and the guide talk history the whole drive down.

I love meeting more Albanians and being around their laid-back nature. As I hear about Albania being conquered over and over again and then being sucked into a communist era, I now suspect why they are so laid back. I even say this to our guide and he laughs saying, "we've been through so much crisis that nothing seems to bother or shock us."

Learning about the country's history, makes me recall my college days of art history. The storytelling and tribal knowledge that is passed down. Our guide, Celi, does it with ease. In Durrës, Albania you can find an amphitheater that used to hold 20,000 people. It was created by the Romans in the 2nd century. Later, the Ottoman Turks filled it in with dirt or some say it was covered by huge tidal waves. Researchers knew there was an amphitheater somewhere in the city. It was on record, but they couldn't locate it. Instead, sat this big hill with homes built on it. Crazy. Celi tells us about a man who unearthed a relic while gardening and then told the city about it. This amphitheater is what laid underneath. There are still parts underground. The houses in the distance won't sell their property to unearth the rest of this ancient treasure. Standing in front of it, I can imagine the gladiators that battled while the leaders sat high up in the carved-out spaces; away from potential assassinations. Celi goes on to explain that they didn't battle to the death because it took too much time to train a gladiator. Most gladiators died from an infection after being wounded. However, thieves were given the opportunity to delay their death with a chance. Beat three gladiators and you can be free. What a manipulation.

We are all covered in sweat from the intense summer heat and humidity, but want to learn more. It's time to get back in the car for more talking and air conditioning. He drives us down to the promenade, the smell of fish hangs in the air. My heart sinks thinking this is the beach. Celi assures me there is more, but wants to give us a tour of Durrës. In the distance, I see an older man in a speedo fishing on his own with a small net. Witnessing his focus was worth the price of admission. The kids are antsy. I want to hop in the water too, but Celi tells us this isn't the place. Too much sewage comes out here. Ew. Now the guy fishing makes me sad. Celi drives us to the beachfront hotels that have chairs to rent.

We arrive and I am floored. This place lives up to its reputation of being the busiest beach in Europe. People line every inch of the sand. Sean wants to bail immediately, but I can't do that to the kids. They've been so patient. They deserve a beach day. Hell, we all do. We finally find and negotiate a few chairs. I offer to hang back while the kids go cool off with Sean. Celi offers to watch our things, but I'm still not that trusting. It's easily 100 degrees, and the humidity dial is cranked up. Sweat is dripping in all my parts, but I try to relax under this umbrella while I read the book my sister Reyna got me as a goodbye gift.

Thankfully, Sean returns to tap out and switch sooner than I thought. My turn to get in the water. I walk past a cart on wheels with two small hibachi grills barbequing corn over hot charcoals. I see the kids, but to get to the water, I have to wade through the line of hungry tourists in speedos with sunburns. Jackson and Izzy are loving it, but I'm grossed out by the litter floating everywhere. The water is warmer than I expected. Not refreshing at all. Brown too. I put on a good face as we bob up and down in the liquid that resembles a pee bath. The people-watching is highly entertaining though. According to Celi, the beach is packed with Polish and German visitors on holidays.

Finally cooled off, we grab a bite to eat right behind our chairs. The sandy beach ends where the restaurants and hotels begin. Celi helps us order and we learn a bit more Albanian food vocabulary. I manage to order my first real fish meal here. They present me with a plate of fries, salad, and a white meat fish called Koce. About 8 inches long, it takes up much of the plate and the eye is looking at me. Tasting like a fatty and oily cod, I love it and leave nothing on the bone.

Sunbaked, we make our way home. I'm disappointed it wasn't as nice as the pictures I saw online. I wish we'd only spent a dollar each to get out there, but we learned a lot. Especially, to go to any other beach that isn't Durrës. Sean starts work tomorrow. I am nervous for him.

Chapter 6

Unraveling is a form of growth. Don't be afraid.

* Day 39 *

Sean's first day at work = my first day alone at home with the kids. We're getting a morning routine going. First, we take turns pulling the laundry off the dry rack from the balcony and put in another load. I move onto handling all the property management duties and start to outline our new financial tracking. We have three banks now and three currencies. Sean is paid in Euros, but Albania isn't a part of the EU. They have their own currency called Lek. Plus, we are still paying bills in the US and collecting rent money as I manage our properties. It's a lot to keep track of, but with me not working I have plenty of time to take care of it. While I work on that, kids are in the kitchen doing their part. Simple living means more time spent doing chores. The kids are impressing me though. I love seeing Izzy up on a chair while the two of them wash and dry the dishes together. Only a few days here and their level of responsibility is growing and they seem proud of their contribution. Even fighting over who gets to wash vs. dry. I'm sure the novelty will wear off.

On our earlier walks, we discovered a fruit and veggie stand up the street along with many local stores and markets nearby. Outdoor produce stands have always been a favorite of mine. With picking off the vine at the ripest time vs. to prolong shelf life, shopping is a 3-4 times a week occurrence here so we integrate that into our daily routine too. I don't mind because the intensity of the flavor in each fruit and vegetable makes me feel like I've been eating fake produce my entire life. Lastly, setting up the home is still in progress. Claudio was nice enough to come over with his dad last night and move Jackson's bed into the previous renters' old sewing room. Now both kids have their own space. Claudio also left behind a hammer and nails that go into concrete walls. I didn't know there was such a thing. These landlords have been incredible to us so far. Today, we dedicate time towards setting up Izzy's room with anything we managed to bring with us from home. Her pink Hello Kitty pillow case and purple Frozen blanket made by Grandma Joan add splashes of color. I wish I had more to personalize it even further, but she smiles at me when we get her white wooden letters, that form her name, over her bed. The same letters I put up over her crib waiting for her to arrive in this world. Then her crib turned into a bed and now they adorn her new bedroom in Tirana.

Sean's first day ends well, and the kids and I show off our progress with the house. He and I both tear up. Starting to feel like home. We decide to end with a celebratory dinner on Embassy Row. Sean learned of this area from some co-workers when he shared our rough experience of trying to find restaurants in our area. It's full of nice restaurants for foreigners. Gonna take time getting used to being called a foreigner. Sean shares details of his day after cheersing our big steins of beer. He tells us about how nice his staff is and some of them have kids that are around the ages of our kids. This makes me even more excited. We're already building a community. I was invited to a Google doc by one of Sean's Vice Principals. "Kid places Albania." We're all collaborating on what we find and sharing with one another. I can't wait to try it all.

* Day 40 *

I went to bed early last night. A beer or two and I was out by 9:30 pm. Waking up at 6:30 am, I start the morning routine. We are a week living here and Sean is on day two of work. I head to the balcony off the kitchen and catch up on what's happening back at home. Still can't get over starting a new day when everyone else I know is ending their previous day. Sean joins me with his breakfast. In the distance, we see the same people running around this worn down field about 100 yards from our apartment. We chat about how the Albanians want to meet up. Have a coffee. On average, they have 4-6 espressos a day and typically each one is an "experience." Sometimes a 1.5-hour chat and almost always accompanied by smoking cigarettes. Some say it's to be seen in the elite status of leisure and not working in the middle of the day. Others say it's a way to pay 50 cents for coffee and then latch onto the WiFi for hours. I see it as their way of life. The new potential soccer coach for the kids wants to meet us for coffee at 6pm tonight to discuss the details. Not sure what that entails, but we Americans are like, put it in an email. Ha! This change is good.

As Sean finishes up his breakfast, I pull out my laptop and start to write. Music playing wakes up my senses. The kitchen is its own room. My new office with windows and a balcony. I can close the door and not hear the kids watching TV. Sean kisses me goodbye and I look down. I don't want him to see the tears in my eyes. Overwhelmed that my dreams have come true. International living, learning a new culture, and writing again bring on happy tears. I make another cup of coffee then return to my keyboard.

I started writing at a young age. It was mostly poems of heartbreak, but it was my way of processing what I was feeling. I suffered from severe migraines and I wasn't good at verbally sharing. Allowing others to read what I wrote was my unique way of letting people in on the secrets I held in my mind. I gifted my first book of poems to my mom on Christmas morning of my 12th year and the first time I visited my mom's mother in Buffalo, I shared the same book with her. I watched my grandma's expression change on her face as she read my words. She looked at me as I sat across from her and said, "These are a lot of mature words for such a young girl. But they are you. Thank you for sharing yourself." I felt so seen and understood in that moment.

Discussing intimate thoughts wasn't encouraged in the house I grew up in. Everything sat on the surface. Making fun of each other was our style of communication. Perhaps a coping mechanism. I was mocked when I was too sensitive or too serious when I tried to express my emotions. The silencing left me to retreat to my diary. It was a safe place for me to live in and it taught me how to connect to my internal self at a young age. Well, safe until my older brother stole my diary and read it out loud to my sisters. They all had a good laugh that day.

When I was 10 we got a computer. I vowed to write my life story on that thing. It's on floppy disks somewhere. Whether penned in a journal, typed on a typewriter, or composed on a keyboard, I could write for hours. Stream of thought writing is subconscious for me. It taps into places my conscious state can't. Even as an adult, I don't think I can arrive to the same place by talking it out. I need a form of creative expression as a communication tool. A bridge. That is why I find myself coming back to writing when I am struggling. It's a dependable friend.

The kids and I shower and head to their new school to join Sean for lunch. One of Sean's VPs, Susan is the wife of Sean's boss, Alan. We meet them and their kids. Oliver 10, Iris 6, Sarah 5. Each born in a different country. Sara comes straight towards me and starts chatting. Like it's no big deal. She tells me of how much she loves ants. They tickle her. She'd let them crawl on her in Shanghai, but advises me to never let red ants do this. "They are poisonous," she warns. China is where they just moved from. Five years spent on Alan and Susan's last school contract. This is where Sara was born. She tells me her sister Iris was born where the elephants live and Alan steps in to expand and share she's referring to Thailand. I love her immediately. She rattles off a bunch more as we make our way to lunch.

We enter a restaurant we have visited twice in the last few days, but it looks different. Our visits to Le Bon were around dinner time. Empty and no food. Just pastries, coffee, and ice cream. Today is a different story. People everywhere. Smells of sweets and savory. It's like a cafeteria. Hot metal containers of different dishes prepared daily and laid out under glass for you to choose. The agriculture here is incredible, which leads to a large availability of vegetable stews and salads. I am in heaven. We all pick what we want and feast as a family of four for under $20. We could have spent even less. Huge baguette sandwiches are $1.50. All the kids sit together, but in the middle is Sean's other VP, Gillian, with a large inviting smile and the little kid eyes are all engaged. My heart is happy watching her in action.

Both Alan and Susan have to work and they don't have childcare arranged just yet. So, during the day the kids are playing at the school and being watched by the Teaching Assistants. They invite Jackson and Izzy to join them and there is no hesitation. Goodbye mom. I'm left heading back to the house myself.

Wandering the streets, on my 7th day here, I am comfortable. I know exactly where I am and where I'm going. I notice my posture. My shoulders sit lower. I head back to the house. It has been a heat wave. Another 100-degree day, but the air is shifting. There is a slight breeze. We've noticed the clouds roll in during the afternoons, much like Florida. The wind catches in my linen shirt, cooling me down. Unlocking the gate and heading up the stairs I open the door to an empty apartment. This is a first. To be alone. It already seems like this is home. I'm glad I left when I did because 20 minutes later I hear a big boom. Thunder. The sky opens up and starts to rain. Pour. I head to my balcony to touch the rain. It's the first time since we've arrived. Lightning strikes and more thunder. It's over in 30 minutes, but the smell of rain reminds me of the PNW. I turn on Spotify and Max Richter, On the Nature of Daylight, plays. I didn't know the name of the song until now, but this song is an old friend. I'm immediately transported back to my little dance class in Portland, Oregon. My body dancing to the melody. It's as if Tracey Durbin is here with me. I recall the moment she looked me in the eyes and told me I need to stop everything and go write. That she would even let me live in her home, on the farm, to get it out. Sitting with that thought in my head and the reality of this empty apartment all around me, I cry. Thank you Universe. You have a way of showing me things when I need them most.

* Day 41 *

Morning starts. Laundry in. Now a daily ritual of my life. Smaller washer and only so many items can fit on a clothesline at once. Also, noticing we continue to run out of things. Purchasing is a daily ritual here. All the packaging is small enough to carry a bag or two home. Nothing too bulky. Feeding a family of four is challenging. Ingredients are bought day-of, used, and then rinse and repeat. Something that will take adjusting, but I understand it too.

I am openly adopting the ways of normal here. I actually thought I'd be without much of what I was accustomed to at home. That nothing would be in English. No brand labels I could recognize. Spices and ingredients would be new. All of it. I even prepared myself to end my love affair with whiskey. To not eat Asian and Mexican flavors weekly. Call it naïve, but I was wrong. It's all here. The body wash, lotions, and razors I used at home. We have a Mexican restaurant, sorta, down the street. We stumbled upon a Wok restaurant that stir frys whatever you put in a bowl with a variety of Asian sauces we are very familiar with back at home. The execution of the dishes isn't spot on, but enough to feel reminiscent. Last night, after meeting the new soccer coach for the kids, I shopped around in a local grocery store for ingredients to stir fry at home with the veggies I bought from the produce stand up the street. It was delicious. You can live 6000 miles away and still have the comforts from home while embracing new at the same time. A pleasant surprise and lesson that other parts of the world have the same accessibility because there is a demand and global marketing is global marketing.

It's a Friday night. Sean is at a work dinner and it's just me and the kids. After finishing setting up Jackson's bedroom with all the sports pennants he could pack and the blue and white Mariners blanket Grandma Joan made, we have an evening in with a homemade dinner and a movie on Netflix. Not jealous at all that Sean is out entertaining. In fact, I haven't worked (in a salaried position) for 7 weeks. I clarify with a salaried position because I do feel like I'm working in a different capacity. We're early in this, but I don't miss my old job and definitely don't miss entertaining clients at fancy dinners. At least not yet. I'm perfectly content on this couch with my kids. Izzy is snuggling me and Jackson just moved over and snuggled her. Without hesitation, I see Izzy's hand fall on his back. Her little hand patted him to comfort. Tender and automatic. Watching these two grow closer makes this experience all the sweeter. Fully relishing in this squishy couch moment.

* Day 42 *

Being in the kitchen. Cleaning the home. Shopping. Caring for the kids. Arranging family activities. The stay at home role. It's all something I couldn't see myself doing full-time, but here I am, happily doing it. I've always asserted myself outside of the house. To stake claim to the "working mom" status. Besides running the finances, Sean has been the nucleus of the family household. It had to be this way because I traveled 70% of the time. But through this role reversal and removing any preconceived notions I've had, I'm taking on this new life and welcoming the effect it has on me. Right now, I'm property managing, writing a book, and caring for the home. All in moderation. All giving me joy. I feel more well-rounded. My time is split between business brain, creative brain, and a whole lot of heart. Balance.

Gillian offers to tour us around the city today with her son Yaw (6) and daughter Afua (4). All done with a mother's touch. The best pizza in town. The go-to chocolatier for the best gelato. Wide, long, flat boulevards for family biking and rollerblading. Fountains to play in. A large public square with a rotating schedule of events. Circus shows to attend every Saturday and Sunday for 40 cents. Great spots to read. Parks to lounge in with tons of green space and a playground that stretches as far as I can see. Off leash dog areas for when we bring Jazzy back in December. A bowling alley under an incredible place to enjoy lunch outside with waiters that speak English. Tirana seems to have it all.

The heat and humidity are getting to us. The hour walking tour commences at a waterpark with three swimming pools, waterslides, lounge chairs, umbrellas, and two restaurants. Smiles all around. Seems like a lot fun for only 500 Lek or $4.90 USD per person to get in. I typically opt out of getting in the water, but to hell with that today. I jump right in.

Sipping beers I get to know Gillian. She's originally from Vancouver B.C., Canada. Started her international career straight out of college 21 years ago and has been in Tirana for two years. She met her husband Kwado, Yaw and Afua's dad, in Ghana when she worked at a school there. They came to Tirana after abruptly leaving Bangladesh because it wasn't safe anymore. She lost friends in a bombing. Story after story, I'm pulled in. There is no shortage of charisma when it comes to Gillian. It's no wonder she's the drama teacher as well as one of Sean's Vice Principals.

After a few hours of soaking, we make our way to a local American themed bar called Duffs. As we enter, I notice the neighborhood it sits in. I look up and see an older woman looking down from a window above. Head poked out on her folded arms. I wonder what she's thinking. What she's seen from her vantage point. Modern and new on the lower level. Communist structure and older eyes looking down from above. I can't ignore the symbolism. The place is classic Americana. Sports memorabilia everywhere. TVs with soccer games playing. Red leather booths. Knock-off pub style food: burgers, wings, cheesesteak sandwich. Sean and Jackson feel right at home. For a second it feels like we never left.

* Day 43 *

Joan sent me pictures of the sliding door added to the basement bedroom, which means the remodel is complete. Time to turn this thing on and market our new lower level garden view apartment. Brian Chesky created something pretty great and started a whole new market when he flipped the switch on his company in 2008. Much like the rest of the social apps, it is spreading like wildfire and property managers are sprouting up everywhere. Now, I am one of them and I am even doing it from Albania. It will serve as supplemental income for me and fund our international travels. We're also going to use the space when we come into town to visit. Win, Win, Win.

Until now, the basement was a forgotten space. The kids wouldn't even go down there unless I stood at the top of the stairs while they used the restroom. Too scared. As the saying goes, I can't believe I didn't do this sooner. I'm pleased with what was accomplished in 7 weeks. There are many little touches I want to still get done, but it's time to make some money.

Writing the ad for the apartment, I do my best to use my marketing and writing skills to make this a spot worth booking. Plus, I've stayed in my fair share of Airbnb's. I draw on that experience and plug in all the information. Within six hours I have my first booking. Within 48 hours, 11 days are booked. Just like that, I have a part-time job. All these people from all over, stopping into Portland for the first time or just passing through, and I get to be a part of their travels. It's also fun to wake up and realize I just made money while sleeping. Just like Warren Buffett says. A completely new way to think about bringing in household income. Well, new for me.

* Day 44 *

Up at 7am, I respond to my new Airbnb bookings and get to work on preparing for our first arrival. Time to set up a guidebook in the app. Place after place comes to mind. There is so much to do and see around that neighborhood. I spend hours making recommendations. It gives me mixed emotions. Creating itineraries or sharing my favorite go to spots on Instagram and Yelp is a hobby of mine, but listing everything out for the Airbnb renters makes me a bit homesick. Of course, I am still very happy I'm reflecting about my hometown from Tirana, Albania. A slight nostalgia lapse is all. Many good times spent in a place I called home for 12 years.

Coming from a foodie culture, the flavors are another thing that have me longing for home. It's only a week and I'm craving REAL Asian and Mexican food. Time to start learning some recipes and leveraging the local ingredients. When you're out of your element, you want to be comforted by things that feel familiar. Food can be a big healer in this ache. Living in the US, especially in the port cities on the east and west coast, you can taste thousands of flavors and textures from cultures around the world thanks to those who immigrated and wanted a little taste of home. Add to that, elevated versions executed by top chefs, fusions that play off multiple cultures' techniques, or of course there are also complete bastardizations. No matter what the situation, you are presented with a dish and there is a connection. Within an instant, you eat with your eyes, then your taste buds, then your heart. You are transported. From the largest scale of family heritage that dates back thousands of years to the smallest scale of taking one bite and seeing your own mom or dad in front of you. Food is the common ingredient of any family from any background. It's intimate, personal, a reflection of a certain land, and a time-honored tradition born of a need to nourish one another with the produce, protein, spices, and cookery on hand.

Now, some people eat to eat. It doesn't matter what's in front of them. It's simply a means to an end. Get full and stay full. And if it tastes good, all the better. Either they are limited in funds or they just don't appreciate the science, art, and diversity of good food. Food gathers people as it adorns a table, inviting people to sit and stay awhile. It inspires hands and hearts to spend time celebrating the best parts of the ingredients or a passed down recipe. We honor the hunter's, gatherer's, and farmer's dedication to their hard work for their communities. And we all reach to taste a memory. Perhaps parts of our childhood that are shared for generations.

Living away from American cuisine, which is much more than a hamburger and fries, I attempt to cook in an effort to pull my home closer. With my hands, my eyes, my taste, I want to comfort my husband, my kids, and my heart. Because evidently, the way home is through our stomachs.

Tonight, I made red enchilada sauce for the first time. Standing in the kitchen for three hours, I cooked. Nothing out of a can. The house smells amazing. My entire life I've poured enchilada sauce from a can. Never again. Mexican cheese is hard to come by in Albania so I substituted shredded gruyere cheese and was able to find cheddar cheese slices to lay on top. Everyone in the family licks their plates. These are easily the best enchiladas I've ever had.

* Day 45 *

I am finding this whole notion of chores really interesting. Probably because it's becoming my life. Since the kids aren't in school right now, it's their life too. These are skills they haven't developed yet because it's becoming less and less of the norm in the US unless your family still lives on a farm. My kids aren't the only kids not learning basic household chores. I can't speak for other homes, but I think it's pretty common for a kid's schedule to be filled with numerous activities leaving little time for accountability at home. Instead of the summer camps they are accustomed to back in Portland, they are doing the dishes, laundry (which includes putting clothes on and taking off a line outside), grocery shopping, cleaning their rooms, putting away their clean clothes, and taking out the garbage. I like seeing the change in them having these responsibilities. It's also helping us find routine, which makes us feel as though we're living here vs. vacationing. Structure is good.

After Sean gets off work, we meet up with Gillian and her kids once again, but also meet Shannon and Bobby and their two boys Julius (14) and Joe-Ben (11). If you can believe it, Shannon and Bobby are fellow Portland, Oregon natives. They just spent nine years in Vietnam and recently arrived as teachers for Albania College Tirana. Bobby actually taught at the same High School Sean left to come here, although their time at the school didn't overlap. What a small world and now Jackson has an American boy his age to hang out with at school. I look forward to getting to know them more. Why did they leave Oregon? What brought them to Albania? What can their international experience teach us? I bet they are a wealth of knowledge. Surrounded in the summer heat, three families gather around a table at the Taiwan Center overlooking the park. Raising our glasses to a good year, we all say gëzuar.

* Day 46 *

I dropped off the kids to play with Alan and Susan's kids once again. It's been nice seeing how open all of this is for people with families. The fact that you have kids isn't hidden. It's out in the open. It's not a weakness when you need to bring your kids to work with you. Instead, it's a contribution to creating an environment that is pro family. I do love that. Plus, others with kids (top down) feel free to do the same. Another fun realization is once you start working together you've already met their whole family. It's not something that just happens at the summer party. And it's not just the spouse. The kids get to know each other too. Overnight, we start to belong to a community. A work dynamic we're not accustomed to, but wish it were the norm in the US.

Walking home, I take notice of all the gates for each of the properties I pass by. Heavy metal. Colorful shades of all the primary colors. Decorative. A statement piece. Not one is the same. Like a signature. Living in the states, I wasn't a woman who sought out a gated neighborhood to call home. Just isn't my style. But this is different. It's still closed off. Not open or welcoming. However, it feels safe and proud. Territorial. Because it's not closing off a whole community or cul-de-sac dividing the haves and have nots. It's an individual house. Protected, private, and adorned like a palace. I like it.

Walking with the kids, without a car, is a welcomed change, but I still need to find a workout regimen at some point. This afternoon my workout consisted of pop-a-shot, air hockey, and foosball games with Jackson and Izzy. And laughter. Lots of laughter. Watching them happy makes me happy. I can't believe I made those little buggers. The life experiences we're exposing them to is molding them. And they are adapting. This age seems perfect to try something like this. As their mom, it's a relief to know they are adjusting here, but I'm learning this is their way because we raised them to do so. It's fun to watch as they get older.

We're halfway home. The afternoon clouds open up again and pour. Warm rain drops. Reminds me of Hawaii or back east in the summertime. Humidity hanging in the air, but the crack of thunder and lightning breaks the heat for a moment. All around we are surrounded with people holding umbrellas. Not these PNW foreigners. Izzy squeezes my hand harder and I look down at her. She looks up and says with her bright eyes, "I think you made the right decision mom. I like it here." Happily, we walk home together in the rain. No coat or umbrellas needed.

Chapter 7

Honor what makes you feel whole.

* Day 47 *

Officially here for two weeks. Most of our vacations max out at 14 days so this timeframe has shifted my brain even more. I appear settled and I'm still surprised how quick and easy that happened. The expat community has helped with the transition and I am becoming more of a believer that home is wherever my family resides. If I am with them, I am home. Although I have enjoyed the life of leisure, playtime with the kids, and time to write, I know the kids are going back to school in 2 weeks. The house will be empty soon. Property management does stimulate my business brain in some ways, but it's becoming pretty templated. I am doubtful it will be enough for me. In the event that it isn't, I'm going fishing for what's out there work wise. I'm curious if there is a local job that I would want. I open the Google search bar and type, "advertising agencies tirana albania." Lots of results. Dusting off my resume, I make updates and visit a few local ad agency websites. I email my resume to two agencies that have no jobs posted, but one agency is looking for a social media manager. Is that me? After applying, I get anxious. Time to dance in my kitchen. Tracey's dance class warmup pours through me. Without hesitation, I move through the choreography with little thought. Muscle memory. The stretch loosens me. It grounds me. My body feels better, but my mind is still racing.

Meditation through cooking is next on the list. I need a dish that requires a lot of cutting and capitalizes on all this fresh produce I just bought. I decide to make shrimp gumbo. An hour of prep, and a slow cook for three hours. My demeanor is laid back once again. The smell in the house is intoxicating. The local vegetables' bright flavors make the dish even more of a crowd pleaser. It was a good day.

* Day 48 *

Finding time to write, while life continues to settle here, is like a scene from *Stand by Me*. I'm Gordy. My kids notice how weird I get when I write. I can't help it. To make it up to them, we head to the waterpark Gillian introduced us to, Aquadrom. But first, we must conquer getting in a cab and communicating with the driver to get us there safe and sound. We turn a corner and find Yuli waiting for a customer. A man most likely in his early 50s, with dark features and a warm and inviting face. His passenger door is already wide open. I've learned that this is code for being available. We hop in and he motions for me to sit up front. I show him Aquadrom on my phone and he smiles as he asks me if I speak Italian. I tell him no, but share that I speak some Spanish. Somewhere deep in the back of my brain, Spanish from three years in high school and two years in college starts to surface. He and I don't understand everything being spoken, but we're having a good time trying. We are laughing with big grins across our faces as we navigate a conversation with broken English, Albanian, Spanish, and Italian. He's full of energy and his attention to the conversation is making me fear his driving a bit. Weaving in and out of traffic, I learn his name, that he is Albanian, and that he has three kids who speak great English. I share my name and that we're American, which did not come as a surprise to him. He then asks me if Izzy and Jackson are my kids. I tell him I'm their mom and then share their ages. I also explain that we have moved here and that my husband works at Albania College. The expression on Yuli's face tells me he understands. With the possibility of me becoming a regular customer, he asks that I put his number in my phone to call on him in the future. In Italian and hand gestures, he helps me type the number into my phone correctly. I just need to give him a 30 minute notice via text, and he will be there. I translate this all back to the kids so they know what we're saying. Jackson, from the backseat, starts to crack up. He's never heard me speak another language. Broken or fluent. Being so close to Italy, many people speak Italian here. I guess I have some work to do. Much easier than speaking Albanian.

We arrive at the pool 10 minutes later and say our goodbyes to Yuli. Mission accomplished. This is our second time here, but a first for just the three of us together. Last time we hung out on the kiddie pool side because Yaw and Afia are still learning to swim. This time we sit on the deeper pool side that has a three-story tall waterslide. The kids talk me into getting them wristbands to ride the slide, but it wasn't a hard sell. They're preoccupied climbing up the waterslide over and over again while I lay out, read, and people watch. A great way to spend a Friday afternoon. Around 3pm another set of clouds come in and before we know it, rain settles in once again. We hop out of the pool, pack up, and head to grab a taxi home. Not enough notice to call on Yuli.

We meet up with Sean and have a fun night out eating pizza while meeting the new school staff who have flown in the last few days. So much English being spoken. I forget where we are. We see familiar faces. Joe, Gillian, Bobby, Shannon, and their two boys. We learn that Joe-Ben will be in the same class as Jackson. Such good news for both families. Although Joe-Ben's parents are from Oregon, he's only known Vietnam as home. Much like Jackson, this is a bit of an adjustment for him. I hope the two of them hit it off long term. To help that bond, Sean and I invite the family back to the house for some Xbox play while the adults share a bottle of wine. Kid giggles and adult story sharing go well together. Our first house party. Hopefully, many more to come.

* Day 49 *

Lazy morning led to an evening of socializing once again with more new teaching staff. Every day someone else is coming into town and the school puts on these gatherings to get to know each other better. Sean heard there is a soccer game happening after the dinner. He and a few other staff members make the decision to give it a go. After a traditional Albanian Zagara feast of grilled meats and vegetables, french fries and salads we head out to our first soccer game in Albania. Shannon, Bobby and their boys meet up with us. Walking the streets, I'm starting to understand the culture of coming out when the sun starts to go down. The air is much cooler and the colors on the buildings are vibrant in the setting sun. The town is alive. It's Saturday night. We're all excited for some family entertainment.

As we get closer to the stadium and pass Woodrow Wilson Square, you can feel the energy of game night. A bunch of 20-somethings dressed in KF Tirana colors are stacked up in a group chanting and strutting down the street. Arms pumping in the air. We're about 15 minutes from game time. We turn the corner and head straight to buy tickets after walking past four different coffee shops. Cigarette smoke blown in our face. I see the ticket booth, but I'm not sure of this line. About 50 men are crowding the sidewalk and pushing their way to the front of the "line." Truth is, there is no line. It's a bee swarm. Biggest jerk with the hardest push gets himself to the window that is fenced off with rod iron. Protection? You put your arms through the bars, but a bunch of other arms are doing the same. Lek bills waving everywhere in the air, you're lucky if they choose you. You grab your tickets and then do your best to use your elbows to push your way out of the crowd. What a mess. What a liability. Is this for real?

One of Sean's co-workers, a man in his 60s, offers to give it a shot and buy tickets on behalf of all of us. I'm afraid for him, but he insists. I'm not sure how he does it, but within 10 minutes he's handing us all a ticket and telling us about his experience. This lack of order is insane. I'm just glad he didn't get injured.

With tickets in hand, we head to the next bee swarm to get in the stadium. Street vendors line the sidewalk with bottles of water and white papers stapled together into cone shapes. The cones are filled with roasted black sunflower seeds. I heard there were no concessions in the stadium. This must be it. We just ate and are anxious to get in so we skip getting food and drink.

A tunnel with steps leads to two turnstiles scanning the tickets to release you from the crowd. We are at the top of the steps, but the crowd isn't moving. Seems the turnstiles aren't rotating fast enough and these fans aren't happy about it. I get motioned into the small gap that has formed. I'm holding Jackson's hand and I look Sean in the eyes and tell him, "Keep an eye on Izzy. Do not stop shielding her from these men." Because that's all there were. Lots and lots of men and you can feel the eagerness of male testosterone. Feeling the breath of male strangers on my neck makes me so uncomfortable.

I try to keep the mood playful. Saying things like, "What an experience. I guess this is the way they do it here. Looks like the game is about to begin. Let's join in and squeeze our way through to the front like everyone else. When in Rome." That's when I notice it. The energy shift. You can feel the frustration all around. Some start jumping up and down whistling. Whites of the eyes are bigger. Angrier. We put Izzy on Sean's shoulders to make sure she doesn't get trampled. The push becomes harder and Jackson and I are in the middle of it. The game starts. I go in complete survival mode and I reserve my bad-mom-guilt-lashing until we get through this. This is not what we expected. A guy notices there's actually a woman in the mix and encourages the men to let me through. Thankfully they start to part, but I'm dragging Jackson with me, a boy just out of the 5th grade among all these men. There is hesitancy about allowing Jackson too, but I insist we both get through safely. Our friends, Sean and Izzy are still in the crowd. I manage to have Izzy helped over the gate and placed in my arms. I lose Sean to the crowd. It's getting dangerous and his instinct is to move his way back up until the crowd clears. The kids are crying and I'm genuinely scared. He messages me on his phone that he is safe. I show the kids the message, but Izzy is still crying for her dad.

Shannon's family makes it through. Shaken up, I convince everyone to find a seat.

10 minutes after the game starts, they decide to open up the entire gate and Sean joins us with wall debris on his shirt. Still in a state of shock, we do our best to be playful in our tone to get the yucky feeling from our stomachs. That could have been really bad. You hear about people dying from stampedes all the time. Where did we move to?

The field is in ok shape and the stands are less than 50% full. Fully outside you can see the sun setting over downtown with a few humidity clouds hanging. Besides the green of the turf, everything else looks drab. No flashy signage. No vendors walking up and down selling cotton candy. No vendors at all. Just a field and dingy partially broken seats with dirt and turf residue. How is this a professional league? I've seen high school athletes with a better touch on the ball.

One of Sean's teachers, Ian, decides to head down to the fan section to get up close and personal to the scene. I show interest and he lets me join. As we get closer to the section, the intensity increases. Walking on the ground level of the stadium next to the field, there are hundreds of male eyes looking down on me. That male gaze. The chanting of T-I-RONA building momentum. It makes me sick to my stomach. I want to go back immediately. Even Ian feels a little uncomfortable.

90th minute goal makes the final score 0-1. KF Tirana loses and FK Kamza wins. Smoke bombs and flares are let off in the stands. Water bottles are thrown on the field. Angry men, all around us, are shouting lewd remarks in Albanian about the player's mothers. We all left with a bruised impression of this country. I guess sport spectating isn't for families in Albania. Lesson learned, but I think we traumatized the kids. This was our first experience of not feeling safe here. It's something I don't want to feel again.

* Day 50 *

It's Sunday. We're all trying to recover from last night's events. What better way to shake off a near trampling catastrophe than a hike in Dajti mountains? Time to redeem our parenting choices. Fresh air. Nature. New terrain. I've been waiting for this all week. Jackson's soon to be homeroom teacher, Todd, offered to show us a place he found two weeks ago. Even drive us in his Jeep. It took him over a year of living in Tirana to find this place and we get to reap the reward a few weeks in.

As the elevation starts to change and we're making our way out of the city, the stillness is apparent. The energy of Tirana can be overwhelming at times. We even live in a quiet spot of the city, but the food and social scene is lined with people and honking car traffic. As the August days whittle down, the population grows as more people come back from summer break. With Todd at the wheel, we slowly take winding roads on our way to Ujevara e Shen Pjetrit (Shengjergj).

A good mix of classic rock is playing on the radio, the windows are rolled down, and I'm in the back with Jackson and Izzy taking in the scenery of the dramatic terrain of Dajti. We pull over at one of the reservoirs. There's the milky blue green color again. It looks even more pronounced sitting at the base of weaving mountain tops. Jackson turns around to find two herding dogs pop out along with eight or nine goats and a herder. Enamored, he quickly grabs his phone to take pictures and I do the same. Not something we see every day. Or maybe we will? The higher elevation means cooler temperatures. It's still warm, but the slight breeze has a little chill to it. It's nice.

We navigate our way to the hike's starting point. Barely anyone is on the trail. Todd leads the way and being in the trees again has me noticing my mood. The vegetation is a lot like Californian mountains near the sea. Dense shrubbery and low trees make everything appear green. A stream and small waterfalls line the path on the way to Erzen river. Of course, the kids can't wait to put their feet in the water. Todd urges their patience because a little further is a natural swimming hole. This news puts a pace in everyone's step. All the water we've been in has been so warm because the sun is that hot. Time for some cold mountain water. The path curves and reveals large boulders outlining swimming pools that are the milky color of glacier water. Everyone races to cannonball first.

The boulders are warm and make for a great sunbathing spot. I do get half of my body in the water for a little while, but I don't like to be cold. Happiness is written across everyone's faces. Splash after splash all four keep jumping in. We notice a few people on the trail. They pass by with looks of shock that we're in the water. Too cold for Albanians. More room for us. Ha!

It's not easy to convince the kids to move on, but Todd reminds us that we're not at the main waterfall yet. There is more and I want to get there before afternoon tour groups start showing up. Everyone takes one last jump in the pool and back on the trail we go. The path onward is pretty sketchy with soft loose dirt. It would probably be roped off as unsafe and inaccessible in the US. As we're scaling the face of the mountain by holding onto tree branches, an older woman in black heeled shoes makes her way down this 45-degree pitch with no problem. A man has a small child in his arms and he's practically running down. The sight of these individuals gives me more courage and I help the kids get up. Part of the path is washed out so we even jump a gap.

We make the final turn and you can hear the waterfall before you see it. This swimming pool is even bigger and the Gropa Mountain water rushes from a mouth nearly 100 feet high. As we get closer, we notice the rock layers of the mountain are one inch slates stacked on top of one another in shades of white, pink, orange and deep red. The slates are so thin you can see where some fell and shattered on the ground in pieces. Time made this. It's hard to believe this place was discovered less than a decade ago. Truly breathtaking. Hiking and nature tours are only recently picking up, but mostly with tourists.

Many Albanians will spend their whole life in Tirana without venturing into this area. We've been told on a few occasions that Albanians think only poor people spend time in nature.

When we arrive, there is a group of people already standing at the base of the waterfall. And for the next hour that we swim in the water, there is a solid flow of tourists. One after one, we witness selfie posing at its finest. Full face of makeup, women line up to get the shot that will make them instafamous. Meanwhile, Sean and the kids take turns sitting under the waterfall. Too cold for me, but highly entertaining. Tourists are even taking pictures of them. No one is really stopping to notice the colorful layers of the rock formation. The picture in front of the waterfall is their only focus and then they head back down the trail. It's starting to gnaw at me. Time to go.

Instead of taking the same "path" back, we decide to meander down the stream. Stepping over boulders, we turn on our problem-solving brains trying not to get our feet stuck in between the rocks. The kids are loving it and so am I. Just enough body in and out of the water and it turned this only 20 minute hike into some kind of a water workout. We make it down safely and we're starved. Todd knows just the place to take us.

Going back the way we came, he introduces us to a spot he likes to go. The views are incredible. It's around 2pm and no other customers but us are in this 3-story restaurant. Feels fishy. Many restaurants here act as a front for the money laundering supporting the illegal cannabis industry. In 2016, Albania became the largest producer of outdoor-grown cannabis in Europe. Nicknamed as "green gold" for struggling farmers. In the second poorest nation in Europe, it's a billion-euro industry. Cannabis isn't the only thing. According to a SkyNews story posted on November 19, 2018 written by Dan Whitehead:

> The deputy director of the National Crime Agency, Tom Dowdall, says the groups are particularly resilient to law enforcement. He said: "Albanian organised criminal gangs are operating at the higher end of sophistication and are certainly operating in the UK as they do within several other countries in western

Europe. They are what we call 'poly-criminals' as well, so not only are they involved in organised immigration crime and trafficking but also in drug smuggling, firearms trafficking and often violent and serious organised crime."

We discuss this topic with Todd while we have lunch. A rated G version for the kids' ears. The corruption and crime is the ugly underbelly of this beautiful place. It's holding the country back from the growth and progress citizens want to see. More Albanians live outside the country than inside. Sure, this is due to the fall of communism, but even 30 years later the country's potential migration has grown from 44 percent in 2007 to 52 percent in 2018. An interesting thought as us expats, who chose to move here, finish a great meal on the terrace alone with jaw dropping scenic views. Todd gets us home all sleepy and thankful for the escape.

* Day 51 *

With extreme highs come extreme lows. Yesterday was amazing, but all good things must come to an end. It's Monday and Sean took the kids with him to hang with the TAs and other kids. I am home alone missing the companionship of friends and coworkers. I miss dance class. I miss the chaos of the office and that makes me feel like a loser. Many people would kill for this life, but I don't like to be idle and I definitely don't like a predictable day. This entire experience has been a series of roller coaster rides. I poured much of myself into organizing everything to get here, I think it's now taking a toll. Sinking in. Even feeling symptoms of postpartum depression. That was a big life event. My days were entirely consumed with the house remodel, packing, purging, saying goodbye, etc. Now, not much else. Empty. This sounds stupid, but I can't seem to find good whiskey or wine to at least get drunk to deal with all this. School starts in two weeks. I'm sure it will be different when that happens. I hope.

I get a message from Sean. Turns out he's having a low day too. Whenever he had a bad day at work, I'd come home to him grilling and drinking beer on the back deck. I get an idea, but first I need to pick up the kids from the school. We head to the local mall to a store called Conad where I'd seen these chintzy one or two-time use throw away grills. I pick one up along with everything to make hamburgers and fries. A six pack of beer added to that and I now have the makings of what turns around my husband's bad work days. We walk home excited to surprise him, but in the back of my mind I'm hoping this cheap grill actually works.

It might sound weird, but in this marriage asking your partner to cook dinner after a tough day is sometimes a good thing. Sean has a connection to grilling. I know not all men do, but a lot feel the same. We set it up on the small table we have on the balcony off the kitchen. To our surprise, the little thing puts a good char on the burgers and for a small moment Sean finds his connection to home. The day ends on a high note.

Chapter 8

When you can't move your mind, move your body.

* Day 52 *

Okay. I have to get out of this house. I'm taking the kids to Aquadrom once again. It's not the refreshing natural pools in the mountains, but it's close, it's easy, and it's damn hot out. With this being my third visit, I think I have this thing down. I assume the position in a lounge chair under an umbrella near the waterslide and the kids pay for their wrist bands by themselves. I sunbathe and book read, while the kids are entertained by the slide and pool for at least two to three hours before they get hungry.

The kids are having a great time. Almost too much fun. You can hear them talk and laugh throughout the entire place. Are we the cliché loud Americans? Standing on top of what is probably a 50-foot-tall water slide, Jackson and Izzy are shouting down to me. They buddied up with a few English-speaking tourists from Germany. Not sure whose idea, most likely Jackson's, but they want me to time them going down the slide. A race. Well, there goes my quiet reading time. I comply and Jackson shouts, "1,2,3, GO!" Oh boy. I let them all go through once. After each kid finishes, I relay back their times. One round through is where it ends. I have to stop it. It's all too loud and I'm always self-conscious about being the loud Americans.

Just as I think I'm going back to my reading, I notice a group of young girls maybe 15 or 16 years old. The instafamous trend is back. A full-on photoshoot is about to take place. Three girls taking turns posing each other in some provocative way as picture after picture is taken. The culture of being seen is out of control here. Fashion and looks seem to be very important to the women in Albania. I realize this is a global trend too, but it appears to be more pronounced here. Plastic surgery is even popular. I see women walk around the streets with their heads held high that they are bandaged up after a nose job. Pride on their face because they can afford such a procedure. There is a beauty shop on every corner. Hair, nails, eyelashes, and eyebrows are always on point. And lots of makeup and perfume. It feels very southern California circa 1999. I'm new to all this and I'm not judging. Simply observing what seems to be a distraction. Hours dedicated to outward appearances means something has to be sacrificed. Relationships. Career path. Financial worth. Self-esteem. I'm not sure which, but it's an epidemic. I see the extremes in the world today. Full-on feminist and activist for change to 10 instastories a day girl trying to be the next YouTube overnight sensation. The pull to be famous is stronger than ever these days. Oy. I feel old. Time to get back to my book.

The last time we were here, the clouds rolled in and opened up a huge rainstorm that lasted about 30 minutes. This time we are prepared with a plan. The first drops start to fall, and one by one people get out of the pool. Now it's pouring hard. The kids and I jump in and swim under the water. There are no rules preventing us from staying. We have the whole pool to ourselves. I'm doing laps listening to the rain fall on the water while submerged. An incredible sensation. Meditative. Floating there, weightless, I am at peace. The novelty of the situation has planted a smile across all of our faces.

* Day 53 *

Day in the life. Wake up. Check Airbnb reservations. Throw a load of wash in. Write a little bit. Make coffee. Cook meal. Clean up meal. Put laundry on the line. Take out the trash. Cook meal. Write a little bit. Clean meal. Think about what to cook for dinner with the limited ingredients I have at my disposal. Shop. Cook meal. Clean up meal. 30 min of snuggles on the couch. Bedtime kid routine. Sing songs. Kiss kids goodnight. Give them a dream to think about as they drift off to sleep. Check Airbnb reservations. An hour of some Netflix show about food. Go to bed. That's it. And it's driving me mad.

Yes, life is meant to have some measurable mundane, but this is not me. Is this anyone? Can anyone find happiness in this? Not a single one of my three emails have been answered regarding job prospecting. I need to try harder. I am counting down the days to when the kids go to school. Sean used to do that when he worked as a teacher and had summers off with the kids. 12 days till the first day of school. I'm in the final stretch. That is why the sound of "mommy" or having to coach Izzy through the completion of yet another meal she won't actually finish is hard to stomach. I'm being the good wife. The good mother. And I can't find why it's good. Oh, and I seem to have arthritis in my left middle finger. Isn't that life laughing at me?

* Day 54 *

Ok. It's a new day. If I've learned anything over the years, it's that you are the maker of your own happiness. If I feel down, I also have the power to change it. I got some music from my dance teacher to complete the whole class. After throwing in a load of wash and responding to two new Airbnb bookings, I give myself a dance class in my kitchen once again. But this time it's the full class. I can't think of a time when moving my body hasn't improved my mood. While dancing, I notice how badly I need to clean these floors. I mentally add that to the list without a grunt. See. Attitude adjusted.

Today, we head to the embassy to start the process of applying for residency. More paperwork and they run a background check. But first, making another cup of coffee and sending out my CV to more agencies and corresponding with the Expat Albania Facebook group for wine bar suggestions. Two things that make me happy. Ding. I receive an email notification. I got a response from one of the agencies. There seems to be some interest in working with me in a small salary/commission capacity. Success! I respond back right away. Even though it's not a signed contract for work, I'm feeling celebratory for a lot of reasons. We head back to the Taiwan Center for dinner and drinks.

When we arrive, Jackson notices the same group of kids playing soccer in the park that he saw the last time we were here. I can see his wheels turning in his head. He wants to play. Asking to be included is something I've been working on with him since he was a toddler. He is a lot like me. It's not his comfort zone. We encourage him to go check out the scene. This means being brave and asking to join 30 Albanian boys for a game of soccer in the park under the moon. It's a big moment for him. After 10 or 15 minutes, I send Izzy to spy. They are playing around the corner from our table, making us unable to see what's happening. She runs back and tells me that Jackson is standing on the sidelines watching. A few minutes later, he comes back. Sitting in his chair, he looks defeated. He was told "no" by some kid. He takes a sip of his 7-up and I say, "So what. What are you doing back here? All it takes is one kid out of 30 to say yes. When a ball goes out of bounds, chase and get it. See what happens." He shrugs his shoulders and I can see the courage build. He goes back out there and I sneak over five minutes later. All of them are only speaking Albanian, but one boy speaks a little English and pulled him in to play goalie. I mom stalk him for a minute, but then leave him to do his thing. 30 minutes later, he's sitting in the same chair, all sweaty, with a confidence I haven't seen before. That night, he came back to the dinner table a new boy.

* Day 55 *

Sitting outside last night at the Taiwan Center, I felt like we were home. Not vacation, but truly living. I needed to get out of the house and it helped a ton. Warm summer night air, people out and about everywhere, and the company of my family. I stayed up late last night on a high. Plus, I was making sure our first Airbnb renter didn't message me for something. The anxiety has me waking up every two hours, but I slept in 'till 9:30 am. Feel good. Groggy with a cup of coffee in hand, I handle all the logistics with the Airbnb and our finances. I also arrange to have Shannon and Bobby's kids join me with my kids. We spend the afternoon at the local bowling alley. Izzy beats all three boys and it's hilarious because the ball rolls so slowly down the lane. To finish the afternoon off right, I buy them each a double scoop of gelato and we people-watch in the park before we head to the last school staff meet-up, again at the American style bar, Duffs. I sip on over-sweetened mojitos and socialize. I'm trying. I nearly fall asleep in the cab on the way home.

Chapter 9

A change of scenery can be exactly what you need.

* Day 56 *

Down day. I let the kids play on their devices most of the day, while I wallow in it. I miss home. The way the water tastes out of the tap. Wine. Whiskey. Beer. Food. Friends. Family. Sights. Smells. It's normal. I am supposed to meet up for a ladies night tonight, but I'm opting out. Can't shake this funk. That's probably the best time to go, but can't peel myself off the couch. These highs and lows. Annoying. Ever since the Airbnb started, I haven't been able to sleep. Afraid some catastrophe is going to arise, but so far nothing. Two renters down and another in progress today. Will the quiet continue?

* Day 57 *

I am straight up addicted. Even more than I was at home. I am constantly checking on people's lives through Facebook and Instagram. I know it isn't a real portrayal of what's really going on in their life, but I can't help it. Forgiveness with my obsession is needed though. I still feel isolated. I'll get there, but when the world starts to wake up over there, I get excited again. What else will they post? I'm actually watching instastories for the first time. Desperate times call for desperate measures. I can't tell if they make me feel better or if I feel worse afterwards. They are empty. Like small talk. The filters, boomerangs of a drink pouring, and cutesy stickers count for my exposure to creativity for the day. The turned around selfie mode for a video makes me extra nauseous. It's like watching someone check herself out in a mirror. The head tilt and pursed lips. No one wants to see that. How can it feel real if the whole time you're talking to me you can see yourself? Maybe knocking on 40 has me turning into an old curmudgeon.

Following Facebook groups like Digital Nomads Around the World, Wordschoolers, Expats in Albania, and Local and International Women of Albania have me sucked into a vortex. Belonging to these groups is a great resource, but it can also be like crack. Well, I have never done crack, but I assume this addiction is a close comparison. At all hours of the day someone is posting, a thread is growing, recommendations are being thrown around, and another family is planning a trip to somewhere in the world. And if I create a post of my own or comment on someone else's the notifications continue to flood in. Moderation is possible, limiting of alerts can be done, but the noise has filled the void of what was work. I think. It's bad. I need to turn it off. It's distracting. I'm weak. How sad that this is my sense of belonging and purpose. Of course, there are things right in front of me that should do this for me, but my brain is conditioned that it must happen in the digital space. Ugly. I don't like it.

The kids start school a week from now. Even though I now have a cold and my entertainment energy is low, I should make an attempt to create a good time. Morning rain has me moving slow and enjoying my typing rant in silence. Seeing everyone in the US post pictures of their kid's first day of school today is rough. Not going to leave the house for a while.

Ending the day hitting up our local mini mart for some water. I watch as the woman at the "register" (a notepad, pencil, and a calculator) interacts with a kid. He's about seven years of age. She offers him two pieces of candy only for him to deny it and ask for cigarettes instead. The lady doesn't even blink. She grabs a pack, opens it up, pulls out two cigarettes and the kid goes scurrying off. What just happened? I can only hope those weren't for him.

* Day 58 *

THE KIDS ARE DRIVING ME NUTS. SEND HELP. School and soccer start in a few days and I'm now counting down the hours. Like most parents at the end of the summer, I've hit a wall. I'm not sure what else to do to fill the days and it feels like we're spending a fortune to entertain them.

Tonight, we are having an Italian dinner with a local Albanian couple, Elsa and Albert. Sean met them through the Albanian grandmother of a student he once taught. The universe works in mysterious ways. We meet at the Pyramid of Tirana. We noticed this structure before, but it looks so run down and dangerous that we didn't get too close to it until now. We've seen people of all ages climbing to the top to watch the sunset, but the whole thing makes Sean and me uneasy. The exterior of the building almost appears to be a set of ramps stretching over 18,000 square feet. With all the foot traffic, the material has softened and become slick. Sliding down is common, but it's difficult to stop your momentum.

Albert and Elsa greet us with warm smiles and share a little history on the landmark. In the late 1980s, Enver Hoxha's daughter co-designed the pyramid with her husband as a tribute and museum to her father's legacy. Since Hoxha's death, it's been used for other purposes including being used as a base by NATO during the 1999 Kosovo war. Today, it sits pretty vandalized and recently a new project was announced that would turn the Pyramid into a technology center for the youth. Sitting nearly 70 feet tall it's hard to believe it used to be one of the highest structures in the city. With over a dozen towering skyscrapers, the capital has changed. We walk around the pyramid and follow them to a nearby restaurant.

This is the first time we're hanging out with Albanians that aren't our tour guide. It's such a nice change from hanging out with expats. We thought they would be accompanied by their two kids as well, but seems they stayed home with the grandparents. Jackson and Izzy are a bit bummed, but get engaged in the conversation and are excited the food selection on the menu is all written in English.

Albert and Elsa are in their early 40s. They love good food, whether cooking at home or going out to a nice restaurant. Both of them are teachers and they share stories about the local education system with Sean. We also learn about Albert's love for American history and that he's even working on a book. The conversation is nice and relaxing. I feel like I can ask them anything so I do and they eagerly ask questions about our stay. All four of us take turns sharing anecdotes about living here for nearly a month, but the most poignant moment was when we went to a soccer game with the kids. Albert's and Elsa's face say it all. They are amazed we went to one. Albert explains that it's not a family-friendly place. He also goes on to say husbands don't allow their wives to go because it's not a place for women. I sip hard on the good wine, finally found some, and try not to assert how much I don't like when someone says a woman is not allowed. I'll assume it's lost in translation. The dinner ends with a large assortment of delicious desserts. Everything is just perfection. Honoring the famous Albanian hospitality referred to as *besa*, they kindly pick up the check for a family of four who they just met a few hours ago. Generosity at its finest. I hope we hang out with them again soon, to pick up the next check and get the chance to meet their boys.

* Day 59 *

In honor of summer break soon ending, we have another Aquadrom day. The capital is filling up. The traffic is the busiest I've seen this far. Nonstop honking. It's mind numbing. Why do they need to honk over everything? And I thought New Yorkers were bad. Albanians are way worse. There's a honk for hello, for move, for you go first, for I'm going to go on the sidewalk to get around you, for get out of my way, etc. Crazy traffic makes for even crazier taxi drivers. I think we nearly hit four people and all while George Michael's *Careless Whisper* is playing on the radio. That sexy saxophone! I did my best to contain myself from dying of laughter at the absurdity of it all.

We arrive safely and assume the learned routine. All in all, the sun therapy is good for me, and the kids play with a few boys from London. We hurry home after because tonight I am GOING OUT. Four weeks ago, today, we left for Albania. This is the first time I'm going out by myself without Sean or the kids. Meeting up with an American that has lived in Albania for the last six years after being assigned here for the Peace Corps. I connected with Erin through a girl I used to CrossFit with back in Portland. They were once roller derby acquaintances and stayed in touch on Facebook. I swear we are all connected through someone else and we only realize it when it happens. Erin planned to go back to the US after her last year of the Peace Corps program, but she fell in love with her now husband. The rest is history. Well that's all I know so far. I'm excited to finally see her.

We meet up at a bar for drinks and my new friend Shannon joins us. Erin can easily spot her fellow foreigners. She approaches me immediately. I guess we haven't gotten down the "blending in" factor yet, but she has. Fully done up in makeup with black rimmed glasses and big dark hair, Erin has the Albanian look down. The bar actually has a Portlandia themed drink and more importantly Bulleit Rye. I knew what I wanted. Erin then proceeds to speak Albanian with the waiter for five or so minutes discussing the different wine options. I have no idea what she is saying, but I love her swagger and tone. She has incredible confidence in her Albanian and this girl is from Wyoming. The whole scene has me leaning back and watching. I'm thoroughly entertained. We get our drinks, clink our glasses, and say gëzuar. Most good nights start just like this. No guards were up. I feel like I could just be myself. No judgement. No ear muffs for the kids needed. No avoidance of certain topics because I'm around Sean. Free. I needed this. Stories start flowing. We're loud. Laughter that makes your cheeks and stomach hurt. Yay for getting off the couch!

* Day 60 *

Like every year, getting these kids back into school without storming the aisles, in search of all the school supplies on their list, is unavoidable. I guess some traditions cross oceans. After some asking around, we learn about an even larger mall on the road to Durrës about 15-20 minutes out of the city center. I have a long list of supplies and if the locals are telling me this place has it all, this is where I'm dragging the kids. I have no car. Target and Amazon don't exist here either. Ah! American luxuries.

After an expensive and always eventful taxi ride, we arrive and it feels like an American mall. In addition to the school supplies store, which resembles the Dollar Tree back at home, there's a huge grocery store with many comforts of home. A convenient one-stop shop of produce, protein, housewares, and groceries. I discover Woodford Reserve whiskey, tex-mex ingredients, Asian sauces, a whole salmon on ice, and a bunch of familiar cuts of meat that I know Sean will like. Am I really this excited over groceries? We aren't living an impoverished life, but something about standing in the middle of these big aisles filled floor to ceiling with goods, I thought I'd live without, brings me small joy. I'm taking pictures and sending them to Sean. He can't believe it either. Tirana is much more metropolitan than I thought it would be and selfishly I cling to the accessibility of imports. It's very American of me, I know. The truth looked me right in my face at this moment. I wasn't ready to give it all up.

Knowing we have to haul this all back, I'm choosey about what I buy and leave feeling good knowing it's there. I can't wait to go home and make Indian food with my purchases. And if you were wondering, the bottle of whiskey also made the cut.

* Day 61 *

Before the first day of school, the new kids are invited to attend a student orientation at the school. Jackson's grade level is up first today and the scheduled time is much longer than Izzy's. Although this is their first year at ACT, this isn't the first time the kids have been to the school. I love how they walk in like they own the place. As a parent, it's a nice treat to see confidence in your kid's body language. And it's especially true when it's in a new environment. They haven't even started day one yet and I'm already proud.

While Jackson is at his orientation, I take Izzy over to the mall's kid play area. Alan and Susan's kids are there too. The four of them run around while I sit and get to know their nanny, Alta. She's young. Mid-twenties. She begins, like most Albanians, apologizing for her English. I think her English is fine. Actually, it's great. And she asks how I'm enjoying our stay in Albania. Her facial expressions move from shock, to pride, and to agreement, as I share all the good things we've experienced so far. People have a hard time understanding why a bunch of Americans would want to come live in a country that its own native people want to leave. She and I come from two different worlds, but we settle on the human side of us. We are all searching for something and that something is different for everyone.

She left the country to study, but came back to Albania. She lives in Tirana and not her home village because there is more opportunity here. We dance around a lot of topics in the beginning, but we stay here for the remainder of the kid play time. The disappointment in her eyes along with her frustration is evident. She did everything she was told to do. Got the grades. Studied hard. Paid for expensive education. Received her degree. Then when she came back home to put that degree into a career, there aren't any jobs. Laughing she says, "We have the smartest waiters in the world." She feels duped and she's not alone.

But this isn't just an Albanian thing. I tell her that many young adults feel the same in the US and this surprises her. Her impression is that America is the land of opportunity, and in many ways it is, but college degrees are more common than ever and the school loan debt is incredible with the government underfunding education. Plus, we are a population of 300 million where the competition is fierce. The marketplace is changing dramatically. Out of the Fortune 500 firms from 1955, only 60 remain in 2017. Certain job types are just going away and there is a mad race globally to stay innovative.

Now, I'm not trying to be insensitive or compete with her discontent with her situation. The conversation tone is calm. She is curious. I explain further. We often compare things to try to understand ourselves or our own circumstance. The grass is greener delusion can distract us. Her mood shifts from angst to something a bit lighter. I can tell she feels burned, and she's right to feel that way, but she appears to feel a bit better off than when the conversation started. In my 20s and 30s I experienced a lot of that. The world isn't what you thought it would be or what someone close to you told you it would be, and now what? She seems smart. I encourage her to honor the bitterness and then put it away. Don't let it be what keeps you from moving forward. I'm talking to her, but it felt good to say out loud.

* Day 62 *

Idle. Too much idle. Change of scenery please. Without any planning, I'm booking a rental car. We're getting out of Tirana and going to explore. I don't even care where we go. I just can't sit here pining away writing in this uncomfortable hard chair. We were out late last night, drinking beer with some of the school staff, but I have a rush of motivation. Sean and the kids think I've gone crazy and want to laze about on the couch longer, but I'm calling the shots here. We all need this.

This is the first time we're renting a car here. I booked with Sixt rental cars, but I have no idea where to pick up the car. We pack a few things in our backpacks, put the address into Google Maps, and set out on foot to find the place. The lot is supposed to be a 15 minute walk from our house. It's mid-morning, but the heat is already intense hovering around 86°F. We arrive on the street of the lot, but Google Maps isn't right. Sixt is nowhere to be found. I get the feeling this will be our first of many run ins with incorrect information. Sean's anxiety starts to kick in and that sets off the kids. We're walking up and down this street and see no signage for Sixt. We attempt to call the place and they said they will call us back with someone who speaks English. Five minutes of waiting for the call feels like an hour and Sean wants to call it quits. I'm seriously bummed and we're all drenched in sweat and frustration. Sean's phone rings and I am relieved. The guy on the phone navigates us to the other side of the street, different from what Google says, and through some security gate. All the Sixt signage and the entire lot is tucked in the back. None of it can be seen from the street. There is no way we would have found this place without his help. We were going in circles and all along it was a three minute walk from where we were. I take a seat with the kids and Sean removes his backpack exposing his wet shirt.

We all have sweat rings on our shirts and red faces, but we try to put that behind us. We now have a car. It's a car that appears to be someone's personal car and not a relatively newer model that we're accustomed to when renting a car. The car squeaks like it needs some work, but it has air conditioning and is bigger than what we actually rented. They tell us it's all they have available. Sean and I look at each other, don't ask too many questions, and squeal off to Shkodër or Shkodra in someone's VW Jetta. If Google Maps doesn't fail us again, it should take us less than two hours to reach the castle in town.

We've lived here nearly a month, but this is the first-time Sean is driving us somewhere. I've missed the freedom of going when we want, but I don't miss the expense of owning a car. In the first five minutes of our drive, the reality of what it means to drive in Albania slaps us in the face. It truly has the worst drivers I've ever seen. No adhering to traffic rules, streets without painted lanes, free-for all-attitude, and roundabouts that are a true disaster. It's the wild wild west.

Only 600 cars existed in Albania prior to 1991 and only Party officials were allowed to drive them. The stalled road development was on purpose. The same is true with air strips for helicopters and planes to land and take off. It was a part of Enver Hoxha's communist isolation. When communism fell, automobile ownership skyrocketed.

Cars are at the center of the culture. Not to generalize, but an Albanian told me he'd choose having a nice car over food. Mercedes are everywhere and I'm talking about the newest models. Gas stations are hangout spots with most including a restaurant/bar and some even have a hotel attached. Car washes are on every corner to combat the dirt roads that still exist. Your car is a status symbol even if it's all for show. It's an obsession unlike anything I've ever seen and I have a lot of car loving friends back at home. This is another level.

Sean got his driver's license in 1994. This means he's been driving longer than most of the entire population. The mood is tense on the first roundabout, but we get through safely. Once we get out of Tirana, things feel a bit easier. Less congested. Less noise. More open road in front of us. Some of my best moments have been riding in the passenger seat with Sean on a road trip. He likes to drive and I like to look out the window and daydream. A perfect match. I reach my hand over to his as he puts it in 4th gear and we cruise.

The green vegetation and mountain scenery on the drive is breathtaking. We pass through quite a few small villages that feel like they are in the middle of nowhere. This feels good. Finally getting out and seeing what this country has to offer. It's only a day trip, but we have to start somewhere.

We arrive in Shkodër with teenagers jumping off the local bridges and into the water. I received some recommendations from Erin. Her husband is from Shkodër. We make our way to the Rozafa Castle to explore the grounds and to get the best views of the city. The walls of the fortress date back to the 4th Century BC, over 2400 years ago. Incredible. The oldest castles in Germany, and much of Western Europe, were built in the 7th Century and I thought they were old when I visited.

Before we even enter the castle, we stop at a viewpoint platform and are in awe of the untouched landscapes that surround the city center. Sprawling green lands, little pockets of homes with red roofs, 360 degree mountains that stretch out as far as the eye can see, and a river running through. We make our way in and find the cobblestone paths extra smooth and slippery. Many have walked here before us. We hold hands to brace each other as we tour ourselves around.

I've been to my fair share of castles, and this seems to be a recurring theme. Honoring the integrity of the historical relic, it's often left in its purity. Very few modifications. As I hold onto Sean, I think about retired tourists running a very serious risk from falling. Some of the most beautiful places I've seen in my travels are hidden down some rickety path and I am thankful I've had my youth and strength to explore. Seeing a photo of these places doesn't do it justice. You are limited to what can fit in the frame and what the photographer choses as capture worthy. Gazing from a tour bus to simply snap a photo doesn't suffice, either. Not even the latest virtual reality technology can really take you there. Being somewhere is an experience for all of your senses. The way the air feels against your body. If there is moisture or salt in the wind. The cold of the stone handrail. The magnitude or cramped feeling of a space. The vastness of the layers in the surrounding environments that only your eyes can discern the depth. No start and stop for your eye line. The smells of a damp cave or blooming vegetation. How vivid and rich the colors are in the painting or nature herself. The textures, light, and shadows on different materials. The energy of a past population that once stood in this exact spot. All of it. It's a full body experience creating muscle memory for the sub and conscious state.

As we work our way through the fortress, our tummies start to rumble. We haven't had lunch yet and Yelp doesn't work in Albania. Where is the nearest restaurant? We notice there is actually a restaurant in a portion of the castle that's still very much intact. How often can you say you had a meal in a 4th century BC castle? Let's find out what that's like.

The archway opens to a narrow room of tables and chairs, but the waiter tells us there is a better place to sit. We follow and pass by a small museum and a scene staged for royalty. Taking pictures isn't allowed and standing there, your mind can transcend with the lush reds and fabrics. We make our way to a balcony with glass walls. The space is no bigger than 20 x 20 feet. The air conditioner is weak and the glass is absorbing all the heat. We open a window for air flow and sit to enjoy a decent pizza and then espresso. It is perfect. There is much more ground to cover in Shkodër before we head back. Bye castle.

We head out and make our way to our first Ottoman bridge sighting. Mesi Bridge or in Albanian *Ura e Mesit,* which means "The bridge in the middle" and it does exactly that. It sits in the middle of the village of Mes and the modern world continues around it. Built around the 18th century, traffic no longer goes over the bridge. However, you can walk over and it typically has water running underneath. Too late in the summer for us to spot any water. Just dirt and brush. The New Bridge, yes that is the name, was built next to it for traffic to drive or bike over. The side-by-side is actually a clever and beautiful depiction of old and new. Being able to walk the New Bridge gives many vantage points to observe the intricate design and architecture of the Mesi Bridge. The arch and built in windows make you wonder how it's still standing. We make our way over and now we get to walk back in time. Weeds and grass are growing in the crevasses of the stone. I stand on one side and watch Sean and the kids walk in front of me. Late summer sun is creating a dusty haze around us. Before long they disappear out of my vantage point because where I'm standing sits lower. I hear Izzy call to me. She doesn't like me out of her sight. Careful to not trip on the jagged stone path, I join them on the other side.

Next stop, Lake Skadar. There are many names for the largest lake in Southern Europe that lies on the border of Albania and Montenegro. Also, called Lake Scutari, Lake Shkodër and Lake Shkodra. Whichever name you prefer, the views make for a scenic drive on a warm summer afternoon. The rolling mountains of Montenegro in the distance lure you in as you navigate a small one-lane road used as a two-lane. Luckily, it's low season and very little traffic crosses our path. Windows rolled down and arm stretched out to feel the breeze, my hand flows with the beat of the music. This is the good stuff. We see a fisherman on the water standing in his boat, cattle and sheep grazing along the marshy shore, lavender still in bloom in August because it's the Mediterranean, and the sunlight is turning golden. Trees and mountains reflect off the water. It's so breathtaking, I beg Sean to pull over as I take out my phone to snap a photo. What a scene.

We make it as far out as the B7 restaurant, which is very close to the Montenegro border. We stop and have a drink. It's about 5pm and we've learned Albanians don't usually eat dinner until around 8 or 9pm. Our presence surprises the staff because we're the only ones there. The décor of the place is out of a magazine and I can imagine what it's like in high season. It's a bit of a trek, but worth it. You would never even know it's there. Secluded in a cove with a beachfront property, it feels private and VIP. White chairs, distressed wood table tops with white legs, and olive trees providing shade are all complemented with the views of the flat tranquil waters. We even spot fish jumping. Our plans were to eat dinner here, but coming back on this path in the dark would be pretty risky. We say our goodbyes and thank yous and get back on the road. Before we leave the lake, we catch the sun setting behind the mountains. As we drive in the dark back to Tirana, we call it a successful first road trip in Albania. We have a surprisingly good Thai dinner in the city center and then drive back to our house.

Even though our day already felt full, Sean is determined to get our VPN connected on my computer to watch the college football season opener. It actually works. Sean connects the HDMI cable to our TV and we flip through a few games. Technology is amazing. The buzz of being connected back to home leads us to stay up for our very own University of Oregon Ducks' 2am local time kickoff. I watch the first half and pass out in bed.

* Day 63 *

Groggy from last night, we have to kick ourselves out of bed. We still have the car for a few more hours. To make the most of it, we head to Mega Tek to get Sean's 40th birthday present. The VPN to watch American sports was the first present. And what goes best with a sporting event than meat on a grill? This enormous sprawling store is as if Home Depot and Ikea had a baby. There is only one way through it, much like Ikea, and the temptation to buy is strong with our family after purging almost everything we owned and then inherited a furnished apartment with items I wouldn't pick out. We fight the urge and our focus leads us to a whole BBQ section. Sean spots a propane gas grill like we had back in Portland, but our landlord recommends the charcoal one for safety. We load it up in our cart and get out of there.

Next up, I take Sean to the Spar store in QTU to show him what the kids and I discovered. He is just as blown away as we were, and now with a car we stock up. Special attention is on what we're grilling tonight on our new purchase. As we're checking out, the cashier asks, "You here for vacations?" I always love the plural "vacations." I reply the same as I have to the many who have asked this exact question. "No, we recently moved here." And she replies, "Why?" We all laugh, but she's serious. No Albanian [that I've met yet] can understand why we'd want to come here. With images still fresh in our heads from Shkodër, I try to answer politely, but I can tell she still thinks we're crazy to live here. She gives me the same look that people back at home gave me when I told them I'm moving here.

Our trunk is filled with all our goodies. Time to hit the road. With Sean having a few hours of driving in Albania under his belt and me in the passenger seat, we start to notice a few things. Sean's aggressive style fits right in. There really aren't any rules and everyone drives intensely inconsiderate. He eats it up. Loves it. Or he's making the most of it. I can't tell. Granted we don't feel safe, but you have to be on the offensive in these situations. At least you feel more in control of your fate, but it does a number on your nerves. Always on alert. People will suddenly double park their car in the middle of a busy highway. No biggie, just weave around without even downshifting and almost hit the guy next to you. It's ok. It's Albania. That's the way it's done here.

We return the car and taxi home. Sean takes a nap and I get out the tools Claudio lent us to assemble the grill. In my opinion, if you give someone something disassembled in a box it is not a gift. It's a project. Once assembled, I move it onto the balcony off the kitchen next to our small two person wood table and chairs. It fits like a glove and you can take in the view of Dajti in the distance. We end the weekend with a typical PNW meal. Grilled salmon, homemade macaroni salad, and roasted brussel sprouts. Feeling settled. Definitely took a month. Although it was rough at times, I'm glad we came a whole month before the kids start school. I can't believe it's tomorrow.

Chapter 10

Stillness is a state worth searching for.

* Day 64 *

First day of school! Jackson is so excited. He got up early and was ready before I got out of bed. Izzy is even bubblier than usual. I remember that feeling when I was their age. Couldn't wait to see my friends, use my new school supplies, wear my new clothes, see where I'm sitting in the class, and meet the teachers. But for Jackson and Izzy, this is all new to them. They don't have friends yet, they are in Albania, they are wearing a school uniform, attending a private school for the first time, and the primary language for 87% of the students is Albanian. Who knows what this year will bring, but these two and Sean are all ready to go to see what happens. You can feel the nerves.

To get the school ready for welcoming parents and students, Sean leaves before the us. They have just enough time to call their grandparents and receive well wishes before we leave. Every year they typically have my mom and Sean's parents join for the walk to school. This year it is just me. I can tell this dampens some of the spirit of the morning. I do my best to take lots of pictures to share on WhatsApp and take a little video of our stroll. The confidence in their steps give me this sudden realization that they are ready. Adaptable little buggers. And they look good in the powder blue school shirts. The sun is shining and I'm wearing my sunglasses hiding my proud mom tears. Sean is in the school driveway directing traffic and welcoming everyone. Izzy runs up to him and he picks her up to plant a big kiss on her. Jackson approaches next and they share their made-up bro handshake. I watch and feel comforted by them doing this all together. Under the same roof. A unique situation, offering mornings like these, every school day. I kiss and hug them goodbye and they disappear into the shuffle of the other kids making their way to class.

Now it's just me. I walk home alone under sprinkles of rain that feel timely. Entering the house, the stillness make it seem bigger. The emptiness and outside air makes it feel cooler. I turn the air conditioner off for the first time since we arrived. We had such a long and hot spring and summer. It's strange to feel cold on my skin again. Fall is coming. My arms wrap around my torso to warm me up and to console me. A lot has built up to this moment. Another milestone crossed. I am relieved, but also scared of my future days. Now it's time to focus on getting me a life. Whatever that means.

As I hang up the wet clothes on my new fancy dryer, aka the clothes line on the balcony, the appreciation is there. I went from the director of marketing at a company that sells technology convenience to going back in time to the ordinary life tasks. Time for my hands to do things, to feel like I'm helping myself, giving me much needed breaks from screen time, empty space for my brain to just wander, to slow down life. A way to unwind that doesn't involve booze or some other substance. Just good ol' fashioned line drying clothes and washing and drying the dishes by hand.

Looking back on my 16-year advertising career, marketing for brands like Nike, Adobe, Visa, and Microsoft, it's hard to believe how fast that went. I poured myself into my job and I didn't leave much room for other things, or other people. From eight years old, I was a girl out to prove I could be and do anything I set my mind to. And in a lot of ways I did. Climbing the corporate ladder like so many others, I ran that hamster wheel at top speed. I made a lot of people a lot of money. Subjected my psyche to egregious egos, "mad men" culture, and obscene entertainment for the clientele. 80 hour work weeks were typical and even celebrated. Busy was a badge of honor. Burn out, a milestone. But there are more than a handful of projects I'm really proud of leading and I did meet inspiring people along the way. People that showed me my potential and helped me realize I wasn't so odd. This path introduced me to people like me. It can be incredibly lonely to feel like an outsider. I was a part of agency teams that made me feel whole.

Living this life, Gary Vaynerchuk had me convinced I was a hustla. That this fast paced, money making world is my golden opportunity to get mine. Of course, relationships would be sacrificed in this path to success. Instead of the dad in the 80s that traveled 70% of the time to support the family he never saw, I was that person sipping whiskey and having a hard time looking in the mirror of the airport bathrooms. As I was leaving the US, I watched a video of Gary V interviewing some kid who did one dance, the floss, with a backpack and became a sensation. An influencer. He was consulting him on where to take his 16-year-old career next. Career? What is happening? How is this a career? I wanted to vomit. Come on. Time to get out of the game for now. Maybe return again when it's right side up. For now, I'll be over here hanging up the laundry.

I pick up the kids from their first day and their little bodies are full of energy. They keep cutting each other off trying to tell me about their day. I smile and try to make sense of it all. Today is their first soccer practice too. After a quick snack and change of clothes, I walk them to the complex. As we enter the indoor fields, I see a woman, in a wrap dress, running full speed while barefoot. She's chasing her 7-year-old daughter. I introduce myself to her and her husband. She is Albanian and works for the Albanian-American Development Foundation and her husband is from Salt Lake City, Utah and manages a full-service office design agency. He even mentions that he can introduce me to the managing directors of two big name agencies in town. We get to chatting, exchange information, and I hope we connect again.

* Day 65 *

Day two of school. While Sean and the kids are away, I'm planning another weekend getaway and finalizing Sean's birthday plans for tomorrow. His birthday happens to fall on the same day Albania celebrates St. Mother Teresa day. I didn't know she was Albanian, but it gives everyone the day off. This means two days of school and then a day off. Not a bad way to start a school year. Home alone again, I'm not sure what to do with myself. To keep myself busy I decide to clean and rearrange the entire house. Tired of inheriting how the renter before did things. I want my stamp on things. Then I take a big nap. Because I can.

I get the kids from school and we do our nightly routine. Kids now in bed, Sean and I turn on Netflix. Like clockwork, Sean falls asleep within 30 minutes. I really can't blame him, but of course I yell at him because he's my only adult interaction for the day. It's tiring to work. I didn't work all day. In fact, I haven't worked for two months. I'm not tired. I want adult company. I feel bad that I yelled. I shrug my shoulders and stay up late binging on too much social media. That will take the place of adult companionship, right? Wrong. The truth is I'm bored. Bored and lonely. I'm filling up my time with meaningless crap. Distractions. Ugh... I may be going nuts. I have this blog I've been writing for over two years. I started it to influence positivity in my and other's lives and to get writing again. To be vulnerable when sharing personal stories in an effort to relate to one another. To lift one another up. Documenting moments, that truly influenced my life trajectory, is my path to finding my writing voice and to have a great collection of essays to pass onto my kids. However, every time I post something I obsess and check constantly for responses. Refresh. Refresh. Show me the stats. This positive is turning into a negative. I posted a new feature today, which means I'm extra nutty waiting for validation. Creativity is hard. It can fill me up in the best way, but also make me feel pathetic at the same time. Sharing with others is a part of the process in impacting others' lives through art. While you're waiting for the thumbs up, literally, you begin to doubt. Even feel like a failure. Almost push delete. I then have to remind myself that I'm doing this for me. The "doing" part is the prize.

It just turned midnight. Sean is officially 40. He is in bed and I'm out on the couch. I really should get some sleep. If I don't go to bed, I'll just eat more. Not a good idea. My stomach is in knots. My head hurts. I suppose I should turn in.

* Day 66 *

It's Sean's 40th birthday and I'm doing whatever I can to make this not suck. We used to talk about how big we'd make our 40th birthdays. Joke about renting a private jet with our closest friends. Well, this won't be that, but what can I do? He and I make a big deal out of birthdays every year and especially on decade milestones. Another year alive and together. What's not to celebrate? I know he's depressed about turning 40 already and being away from home isn't making it any easier. I whipped up some crappy chocolate cake yesterday with Izzy, made a bacon and egg breakfast this morning, and arranged for a few of our new friends and their kids to meet us at a local water slide park that is supposed to be better than Aquadrom.

Never in a million years could I have predicted this, but here we are entering the park with 50 Cent playing over the loudspeakers. Although it's supposed to be an 80-degree day, that's cold for Albanians. The place is pretty empty. We have the park to ourselves. We find a group of lounge chairs by the main slides. Kids are already off trying to get as many turns as this day will give them. I order the first round of drinks and we keep them coming all day. I do think it's nice to play like a kid on your 40th, but I tread lightly. Our eyes meet up a few times throughout the day and I can sense he is chalking this up to life experiences. I know the kids are having a blast. Funniest dad birthday EVER. They aren't typically attendees at the birthday festivities besides a family dinner. Jackson even mentions that he is glad he gets to be a part of it this year. I know I'm enjoying watching the two of them race down the water slides cracking up. My boys. Izzy's laugh can be heard from across the park. Her and her friends are pulling on levers to dump buckets of water on their heads. See. It's a great time for all.

We end the evening back at home after a chill bus ride. A little hung over from day drinking, we sing happy birthday without candles. Jackson holds the long lighter for Sean to blow out. Along with not finding a place that sells cakes or cake mix, I couldn't find candles. Even sadder, the cake I made is overcooked. Wife fail. We all pretty much stick with the vanilla ice cream. We video chat with family and I wander over to the couch. I hope he feels celebrated. I tried. Time to call it a day. I'm beat.

* Day 67 *

Kids and Sean are back at school. Down day for me. Been a busy week getting the kids ready for their first day of school, starting soccer for the kids, then Sean's birthday, and a lot of Airbnb stuff. I guess it's ok to feel lazy today. This support woman is taking a time out. Walked around the neighborhood and found a stretch of restaurants near our house that I didn't know were there. Pleasantly surprised. I researched it and found out it was a landing area for helicopters during the communist era. Nice flat and wide stretch of walkway with no stop lights or much traffic. As the air cools, I think it will be a good place to run around.

After yesterday's homesick day, I decide to look for flights back to Portland. Fares over the Christmas break are pretty cheap. I jump at the opportunity and book them. Feels good to have that box checked, but then I have other thoughts creep in too. Sometimes I find myself watching a movie and notice how lived in the homes are. Like they have been living there for ages and the layers of time show in the layers of décor. There are days that I wake up and want that. The one home. The BIG family home where everyone gathers for holidays, after school hang out sessions are a regular thing with the kids, and the banister is perfect for pictures before school dances. Then other days I want nothing but the backpack. The bare minimum. A rental without personal effects. Maybe someone else's but not mine or ours at all. Just being nomadic. The only thing I own is what we're going to do today. Right now, I'm sorta living a hybrid. It has its pros and cons too. I get a healthy pull from both of these worlds when I sit in the middle. Even when I was "settled" in home ownership, let's be honest, I wasn't big on putting my time and energy into my 100-year-old home. I spent more money and time on it once I knew I was leaving it. Plus 90% of the time I inhabited it, I was still living out of a suitcase between travel for work and life; feeding my nomadic nature. But it was our home base. Something to come back to after being away for a period of time. Always on the go, while it stayed exactly in the same place, gave us a sense of stability. Belonging. While everyone and everything was moving around on the earth, it was always there when we needed it. Comfy couch. Bed mattress with the right amount of firm and soft. Kitchen drawers arranged the way our brains are wired. Family photos on the walls. Neighbors we know and love.

This December we'll be visiting Portland as guests for the holidays. The trip is our Christmas present to the kids, to us, and to our extended family. We've been giving experiences as gifts to each other for some time now and this is the biggest one yet. However, our visit is during a time of giving and opening gifts with people that don't share in this tradition. How do you fit in with the gift giving when there's nothing to open? And with our minimalist living, we are unable to fly back with much of anything. How can I feel like a good mom, friend, sister, daughter and not create a feeling of awkwardness each time this tradition presents itself? Not give the kids the Christmas version they want?

We have made a recent life choice and I know it's not for everyone. I am both anxious and excited to surround myself in familiar again and to kiss the faces I've missed so much. Our family home still stands and is owned by us, but others are living in it. We'll only have been gone for a few months, but it already feels like our whole world has been flipped upside down and I have little understanding of what's going on in other's lives. It reminds me of an old Christmas classic, *It's a Wonderful Life*. I'm not saying my good deeds compare to George Bailey's, but I do know this Mailey family has made an imprint in people's lives. And unlike George we're out seeing the world to continue to build our community, learn from others, and widening our friend circle beyond Portland, Oregon. I guess what I fear most is we go home to find a world that exists as if we never did.

Chapter 11

Give it time. You'll see clearer.

* Day 68 *

Home sickness seems to be an epidemic. We're all craving a burger. An American style burger. We head over to HaBurger to get our fix. The burger is just ok and the four of us start describing what makes a burger truly American. An odd topic that somehow leads to the latest news of Nike supporting Colin Kaepernick's decision to take a knee during the National Anthem. Sean is in complete support of it and I beg him to see this another way. To me, this is a PR stunt that appropriates a black man's message to take sexual harassment along with gender and race disparity out of the headlines. I'm sure they'll even win accolades for the campaign. Nearly the same day the commercial was released, Nike was being sued by shareholders over sexual harassment allegations. Five months after a women-led employee revolt outed the inner circle of men who ran the "boys club" culture. Headlines continued to rollout over the summer, but it all stopped when the new '*Just Do It*' ad ran in every media outlet. Men are "just doing it" a little too much, but the giant rebounds. Revered once again and in time for back to school and holiday shopping. No more New York Times coverage about the lawsuit or the 11 or so senior executives that left Nike. In advertising, very little happens by chance. It's been two years since Colin Kaepernick first took a knee and now Nike decides to take a stand all of a sudden? The whole thing is hard to swallow and hits way too close to home. Kaepernick said, "Believe in something. Even if it means sacrificing everything." Who or what was sacrificed in this latest move, Phil Knight?

The silent walk home helped settle my hands from shaking. While Sean and the kids watch something on TV, I keep the trip booking train going to get my mind off things. All plans have been finalized for a weekend in Vlorë tomorrow. Researching the area has me excited. This is our first overnight trip. Found an Airbnb with a beautiful balcony view and the beaches in the pictures look amazing. Can't wait!

* Day 69 *

We pick up the car and this time we know exactly where it is. But because it's always an adventure here, we quickly learn that I ended up renting the tiniest car ever called a Tata. It's a car brand from India and it also comes standard without a radio in the dash. What? I had no idea that I needed to check if a radio was listed in the options. We get Spotify going on Sean's phone while we use Waze to navigate our trip. Technology still works. Phew. Away we go!

The drive south is gorgeous. Mountain ranges are vast and full of green, little villages tucked in here and there, and the most beautiful water I have ever seen. We purposely waited until September to visit after we got a local tip. The place completely empties out as August comes to a close. Too cold for locals and everyone is back to work and school. After a 2-hour drive, we arrive in this beachy town on a perfect 85-degree day. Sean and the kids are eager to jump in the water. I'm eager to sunbathe. We drive past the public beach and using another recommendation we head straight to an area of hotels that rent out chairs on their beachfront property. We find a nice quiet spot with only a handful of guests. Hungry, we sit down to a seafood feast, homemade Raki which is a bit like grappa, and delicious salads. The white porous boulders, colorful umbrellas over the lounge chairs, sea glass and shiny pebble shoreline, and emerald colors of the Aegean Riviera all create a stunning view. To think just two months ago we were driving over two hours to visit Rockaway Beach in Oregon and now we've driven to this place in less time.

The sun is hanging lower in the sky and the wind is picking up. It's hard to pull Sean and the kids out of the water, but it's time to pack up and go find our Airbnb in the olive grove mountains. Finding it is a bit difficult, but we get there. We pass through a gate with about a dozen stray cats and chickens roaming the driveway. The place isn't great, but the views are breathtaking. Typing from this balcony spot is inspiring. The sky is melting into a sunset, downtown Vlorë is in the distance, and the sea is still visible just beyond the shore. Perfection. Sean and the kids come out to join me. We look out until the sun sets and the dark skies replace it. We have a nice dinner in town, ride a few sketchy rides on the promenade, indulge in dessert, and then hit the bed for some much-needed rest.

* Day 70 *

That night of sleep was rough. No air conditioning in the place and the beds were hard as can be. The windows don't have screens, which meant mosquitoes and probably fleas would eat us alive if we opened them. I did turn on the overhead fans for air circulation, but they were dangerously loose. The whole fan swayed around like it was about to fall out and rip us to pieces. I turned it down and the electrical outlet sparked. I move the kids, and I sleep under the danger zone for the rest of the night. Napping on a beach might make up for it.

Another 85-degree day with a slight breeze and I'm stretching on this amazing balcony like all the roaming cats. I used to be big into porches. It was always what I pictured in my dream house. Then one day I got a house with a big front porch and rarely used it. I think I was most attracted to the look. The way it welcomed you home. Now living in an apartment with four balconies and then renting Airbnbs with balcony views, I'm becoming team balcony and ending my love affair with porches. There is something psychological that happens when you start your day looking out and a bit down on the world around you. A vantage point that breeds a feeling of empowerment and strength. Somehow you feel both small and big at the same time. It might be the lack of sleep, but I'm feeling that right now and it feels great.

Time to check out and get a breakfast crepe and coffee before we hit up another beach and then head home. The sun heats up quickly. A few people are out walking the promenade at a slow casual pace. The old men are gathered in groups playing backgammon and chess. The mountains and sea are simply majestic butted up against each other.

We drive the coastline south again to find another lounge spot and this time we luck out even more than yesterday. The place is perfect for kids and best of all this pristine area is empty and I'm loving it. It's like this is all for us. I snap pictures and no one is in the shot. I am walking around a scene fit for a magazine cover. Sean and the kids jump off the rocks into the sea and I have hundreds of lounge areas at my disposal. For the record, this is what my version of heaven looks like. Brightly colored bean bag chairs, beachy grass umbrellas, sand-colored cushioned wood lounge chairs, and even beds with royal blue sheets and white silk curtains hung from above. Between the cloudless sky, open sea and mountains in the distance there are too many shades of blue to count. I don't want to go back home today. My grandma Rosemary Klumpp would approve. She always had a beach chair in the trunk of her car because you never know when life will present a great sunbathing spot. I think about her as I doze off under the heat.

After hours of playing in the water, we are starved. We head into the restaurant to see what they have to eat. With only us and a handful of others we see at the tables, I'm curious what they have to serve during this low season time. Something we've become accustomed to in Albania is the menus are pretty useless. It's probably why they don't even make them available online. When we first arrived in the country, we searched the menus for items we wanted and then sat down. A typical habit when finding a place to eat or so we thought. When the waiter arrived, he'd tell us the dishes we wanted aren't available. Bummed we'd point at other things listed and he'd shake his head 'no' once again. Eventually, we hear verbally from the waiter what they do have available today and pick from these items. At first, it infuriated me, but then I started to get used to it. Albanians cook seasonally and farm to table. It's not to be trendy. It's a way of life. They don't spend the money to have different menus to reflect the changes, but what they serve you is fresh and you can taste the difference. I'd much rather have fresh than an item that is ordered once a month and sits frozen ready to be thawed. The dining experience is more conversational as well. For a first-time visitor who is unaware, I could see this feeling rude and off putting. Something for the restaurant industry to think about as they look to broaden to serve tourists. It has taken getting used to, but I'm prepared when we approach these waiters. We have a great meal overlooking the water and then pack up our things to head home. An incredible weekend getaway that has us falling in love with Albania even more.

* Day 71 *

Back at home. I'm a nerd for data and I'm curious how much we're spending on these vacations. I'm the one who always runs the finances in this family and it's even more so my job in this new family dynamic. With the cost of living being low, our hope was to have the Airbnb rental in the Portland home pay for our travels. By my calculations the profit we're turning is doing just that. It feels satisfying to know this for certain. Like the work and hard push to remodel was all worth it. I feel like running. I lace up my shoes and head out to the promenade I found a few weeks back. The morning air is starting to cool down, but it's still in the 80s. As I'm starting to get my stride, I run past a cow grazing in the grass. What? Another odd experience to add to the list. Oh Albania. I think I'll name her Betty. See you later, Betty.

Running tends to re-energize me. The wheels in my head start turning and ideation feels more natural. I'm going to put myself out there and reach out to the couple I met at Izzy and Jackson's soccer practice. Brandt and Ervisa own G&H Partners. They work with professional organizations who are engaged in capital investment projects for their corporate office spaces. Who knows what will come of it, but I'm ready to find out. If it doesn't turn into a job, I hope it at least introduces me to a community of friends. I know Izzy loves hanging out with their daughter. Two strong girls taking to the field with all the boys. Playing with 7-11 year olds, Izzy is getting challenged for the first time. The look of determination across her face and those pumping elbows when she runs is fun to watch.

* Day 72 *

Ok, with the first email sent yesterday to G&H Partners, I think I'm ready to go broader. I've started creating posts on LinkedIn that market me or at least keep me top of mind. Getting great response so far. Making them mostly about my observations while being here and the advantageous working conditions if someone wanted to hire me. I think it's a smart play, but either way it's fun to create content again. I plan to do a post each week and will continue creating posts for Influence twice a week. Between writing those, managing the Airbnb and our household, and arranging our travel plans I'm keeping pretty busy. I wonder if I'd even have much time for a project. To be honest, this lifestyle has my brain on overdrive. Creativity is flowing. Too many ideas bouncing around in my head. My brain was so focused on solving corporate business problems that I didn't have any room for my own creativity. It's all surfacing at once. I can't get it all out quick enough. Thoughts for my book, posts for Influence, posts for marketing myself on LinkedIn, business ideas, self-reflection on American culture, all of it. Just keeps coming. I'm able to write down some of it, but it's not thoughtful yet. Just trying to get it out to make my head stop hurting. I pop more ibuprofen and keep typing. Maybe all these ideas will go away. I rush to document as much as I can, afraid I will forget them later. It's both thrilling and exhausting at the same time. The firehose is open.

Chapter 12

Trust that the road continues even as it bends out of sight.

* Day 73 *

I'm all dressed up with some place to go. It's been awhile since I wore a blouse, skirt, and heels, but here I go. I head into town to the G&H Partner's office to meet up with Brandt and Ervisa. It's completely casual. A chance for me to get to know them more and for me to share a bit about my professional background. After another Google Maps snafu, I arrive 20 minutes early because it's a lot closer than Google said.

I enter the stylish space and Brandt welcomes me in as we wait for Ervisa to arrive from her other job. Filling the space are contemporary classic lines and color palettes. Brandt has designed the office as a showroom to feature the products he'd recommend to rethink the corporate work setting. Eye candy for me, but very different from what I have seen in Albania. High-end. I'm curious about their marketing value here. Regardless, it creates a great space to talk shop. Well, much better than the stadium seats adjacent to a soccer field where we typically see each other.

Ervisa arrives and we share an hour or two sipping our cappuccinos and swapping career stories. The smile on her face invites me to keep talking and she stops me mid-sentence to ask if I've ever facilitated a corporate training. It catches me off guard, but I'm listening. Not only is she the CEO of G&H Partners, but she also works for AADF, a direct implementation organization focused on the development of a sustainable private sector economy and a democratic society in Albania. She goes on to explain that they are looking for someone to lead a professional development workshop for their annual company retreat. I don't get too much more detail, but I'm interested. I can tell she is younger than me, but we have a lot of similar personality traits. I'd like to work with her somehow. We wrap up the conversation out of pure hunger. It's lunchtime. I could have talked with her all day, but we kiss on either side of the cheeks to say goodbye for now.

I walk to catch a cab buzzing. Adrenaline back in the veins feels good. I'm sure I have a goofy smile across my face. I get dropped back off in my neighborhood. Before home, I stop in at the bread store a block from my house. Living here, I feel like I'm seeing how my grandparents grew up. Simple. No Amazon Go. Shopping from specialty shops, many of them, and meeting people along the way. No one-stop-shop anything and all in my neighborhood. Walking distance from my kitchen. The bread lady, still need to learn her name when I learn more Albanian, grabs a fresh baked bread loaf from the cabinet, slices it with her machine, and bags it up for 80 lek which is about 80 cents. Bread in hand, I notice it's still warm. Before the night ends, I get an invite to meet Ervisa and someone else at AADF tomorrow. I love today.

* Day 74 *

Another business day, another dressy outfit. It's hot outside, but the taxi driver has the air conditioning pumping. He asks me if I'm Italian and I hesitate before I correct him. Felt like a compliment and glad to hear my appearance doesn't scream American. Whatever the reason, his question boosts my confidence. I take the elevator to the 12th floor and meet Ervisa and another woman. Three direct, experienced, and opinionated women now sit around a table to talk business. The meeting is all of 40 minutes and I can sense it's on borrowed time. There is a busy energy around the office, but I stay focused and clearly understand what they need. I can do this. I have done this many times before. This could be my first job in Albania. I scribble down notes as quickly as I can and then the meeting is over. I owe them a proposal by end of day tomorrow. The 3-hour workshop will be held in Florence, Italy. They will pay for me to travel there to lead this session with the entire 30+ company employees including the two CEOs. I've never been to Florence. Other parts of Italy, but not Florence. The workshop also takes place on the first day of Sean's and the kid's weeklong fall break. Whoa. Coincidence? I want this.

* Day 75 *

As soon as I get the kids off to school, I get right to work on my AADF proposal. I dust off my company letterhead and can't believe my first ALIST paying job will be in Tirana, Albania. A company I started two years ago after a senior female leader at Intel advised me to set it up for the day I'd need it. Premeditated brilliance I am thankful for in this moment. Maybe I shouldn't get ahead of myself. I haven't won the project yet. Sean and I discuss the possibility of me winning and if I do we're all going to go to Italy for the break. Fingers crossed. Even if they don't choose me, I am having fun putting it together. I really think I could pull off facilitating a team building and planning workshop. Email sent. Now it's a waiting game.

Within an hour of my proposal submission to AADF, a local agency here in Tirana, Manderina Promotions, reaches out to me. Actually, I've been trying to connect with them for the past two weeks after their initial email response to my generic email with my resume attached. It's been a challenge and then all of a sudden I get a WhatsApp message from Alma, one of the co-founders of the agency. We have a meeting set this Tuesday at 10am. How's that for a Friday of productivity? It all started with my Monday morning run that set the tone for the week. Momentum is a great rush. I want to celebrate. Erin invited me to go dancing with her and few other girls she knows. I decide to take her up on the offer and invite Ervisa to join too. A night out is a perfect distraction, while I wait to hear back on my proposal.

We meet for a coffee before and then head to a place called Temple Bar. They host a Latin Dance night every Wednesday. Latin dancing in Albania? The surprises keep coming. We arrive and the first thing I see is a large 6 x 6 foot gold Buddha statue standing front and center in the outdoor garden. A month ago, I learned that Albania is constitutionally a secular country and that during the communist era they became the only country that banned all religions. Churches and other religious relics were destroyed. You weren't allowed to openly practice any form of religion. I can't dismiss the irony of this decor, but I'm quickly drawn in by the crowd of Albanians salsa dancing.

The dance floor is outside. There is a DJ and laser lights of neon pinks and yellows dance to the beat. The air is still heavy from the warm day. The floor is packed and I stand there watching for a bit. All the steps are there, but it's as if everyone here took a ballroom dance class to learn. It's too clean. Too on their toes. Too uniformed. All the chins are lifted. It's the most proper looking Latin dancing I've ever seen. There's no soul. No sweat. No one is down in their pelvis and low to the ground. Robotic. I need to let it go and stop being such a dance snob. I get a drink and then another to loosen up. Now I'm on the dance floor because I can't help myself. It's a hot summer night and I'm dancing under the stars. My hips are low. I'm leading with my pelvis. My feet are staccato and I don't care who's watching. The dance floor is my true home.

* Day 76 *

This evening I managed to kick Sean out of the house. He needs to get out and hang with some guys. He hasn't done it yet. Last night did me some good, hopefully it will help him too. Ervisa's brother owns a bar that has an IPA on tap from San Diego and they are going to use Sean's VPN to stream the Duck football game on the TV screens. American luxuries I know he misses. I worry about him. Much of what he identifies with are just not here in Albania. Golf, skiing, diverse food, college football, everything to do with sports, craft beer, a good steak, driving a big car, this place has none of it. Sean's personality is soaked in Americana. His 6-foot broad build seems lost. Taking this leap is way out of his comfort zone. I know that and I pushed him anyway. It's good for him.

Sean and I are both Type A, take charge types, but this is the first time I'm driving the agenda of the family. We've lived on his for so long. He took this family to some amazing places over the last decade, but I feel like I lost me along the way. I only had my job as an identifier. A lot was on auto-pilot and saying yes because I was too tired. And I was rarely around to own planning anything out. I didn't see myself in this family or our life. Coming home between work trips, I saw less and less where I was needed. It all worked without me. I became detached. I'd do my best to hide the sad inside or swallow the week's pressures because I only got what felt like minutes to catch up with what's going on in the Mailey Household. Flying out Monday morning, I'd try to make sense of how we got here and if there was a way to fix it. A desperate and dangerous line to tow.

Leaving it all behind and moving out of the country may be what I need to get me back, get us back, but I hope it doesn't break Sean in the process. As we reprogram what living is, I want him to find joy in this experience. He seems resistant and adjusting slower than all of us. Even if tonight isn't great, maybe it can be a sweet temporary distraction. Fingers crossed.

I heard him stumble in around 2am. That's got to be a good sign.

* Day 77 *

Late night for me Friday night. Late night for Sean last night. We're getting ourselves out there. Trying to assimilate. And now, we are tired. Gillian suggested a day of lounging at the pool while the kids swim. Great idea. Nice to just chill in our home neighborhood this weekend. Well, look at that. I just called it home.

* Day 78 *

Monday is here. Today, the public schools open. Walking the kids to school, it's clear the population in town has grown. There's a huge increase in foot and street traffic. The honking of the horns is even louder and more constant. I drop the kids off. Kiss Sean goodbye. Put in my headphones. And start my morning run. Different than Portland, there aren't a lot of people running around in public. Especially women. I've learned from a few Albanian women that it's frowned upon to sweat in public. It's also cultural tribal knowledge that if you let your sweat dry on your skin you will catch a terrible sickness and even die. In a corporate office, you can see women tucking paper napkins or handkerchiefs between their skin and their outfits to catch the sweat.

I mean no disrespect to their beliefs when I run and sweat in public, but it helps me understand why I don't see much of a running community and perhaps why I get the looks I get. Still my favorite, are the looks I get from 3-6 year-old girls. Some of them really stare with their mouths open and follow me with their eyes. As I pass, I can't help but wonder what they are thinking. It reminds me of my daughter. I love watching Izzy and her friend Fiora kick butt on the soccer field with the boys. No holding back. The turf gets them absolutely filthy, hands black, and they surely get their sweat on. Ervisa and I are raising our girls to play.

Still no word from AADF. Time to dig in and run an extra mile.

Chapter 13

Be a catalyst for something great to happen all around you.

* Day 79 *

Fall is a second spring in the Mediterranean. Flowers are blossoming. Fruit is ripening. New light green leaves are stretching out of buds on the tree branches. What a beautiful surprise. Nature is blooming while I feel the same. Three weeks ago, I Googled "advertising agencies in Tirana" and the first 10 returned in the listing got an email from me inquiring about a possible job opportunity. It was a lazy way to start, but it was something. Out of the 10 agencies, Manderina Promotions is the only one that responded. We shared emails back and forth for two weeks, and today I'm cabbing to meet them. I have no expectations and they gave me no hints on what they want help with, but I'm going.

It's 9:45 am. The meeting is at 10:00 am. The cab driver drops me at the address, points randomly in some direction and says a few words in Albanian. I nod as if I understand, but I don't see it anywhere. Ugh. Another Google Maps fail. I've relied so much on GPS the past few years. It gave me independence to come and go on my own, but Albania is a different story. You can't trust it. Sometimes it's right and sometimes it's way off because it relies on data being put in correctly. It's an agency so I'm banking on it being right. I keep looking. I cross the street and my eyes wander all around. I look lost. The coffee shops on both corners are filled with people sitting on the sidewalk smoking their cigarettes. I feel like everyone is looking at the confused American girl. Google Maps says it's right where I am standing, but across the street. Scanning the buildings and storefronts, I look up and there's a tiny sign with the agency name. The most buried thing ever. Looks like it's on the second or third floor of the building above a pizza place, but how do

I get there? Now that I know I'm here, I give them a call. Thankfully, they answer, buzz me in a door, and I make my way up. Time to calm my nerves and gather myself.

We meet for an hour or so. The company is led by two women, Alma and Eva, who started their own agency four years ago when they ran into difficulty finding a job after having kids. They are a small company. Two co-owners and two or three other younger women running the social media channels for their clients. Growth is their goal and I want to help them. For the first time, they are hosting a photography festival in their National Museum of History located in Skanderbeg Square here in Tirana. They need help with finding sponsors or donors, and the event is six weeks away. I know no one here, but this could be a way to change that. When I left Portland, I said I wanted to dedicate my time to helping underserved, under-represented communities and businesses. Even if it meant doing pro bono work. This is the first time in my life, I'm in a financial place that I can make this happen. The festival is a celebration of this new country I'm calling home, it spotlights the art of photography, and I'd be helping Albanian women. With complete confidence, I look them in the eyes and shake their hands. I can help them and I will.

After taking myself to lunch to celebrate, I rush home to change and then pick up the kids from school. I'm on a high from my day. Holding Izzy's hand, we cross the street as Jackson tells us he's going to run for homeroom representative. Student government. Leadership. Just like his momma did. I have a hard time containing my excitement when he shares his news. I don't want to scare him away from this. I play it cool and give mom encouraging words in a calm tone, but I'm bursting inside. He walks right in the house and gets to work on his speech. About 30 minutes later he comes out and reads it to me while I ugly cry. This kid. I'm at a loss for words. Looks like I'm not the only one blooming today.

> *"Hello, my name is Jackson Mailey. You may not know*
> *a lot about me, but I promise you I am the right man*
> *for this job. I am funny, athletic, kind and awesome.*
> *But the two most important things I have for this job is*
> *a listener and a communicator, also fortnite.*

I want to become a communicator more because being a representative you have to communicate a lot. I will bring all your voices and put them into the government. Every single one of you has to have their voices heard in ACT. Everybody is equal in my opinion, no matter who you are or what you think. I will respect every single opinion you make.

I'm not just an activist, not just your fellow representatives are leaders, we all are. We are one big voice and I am putting myself out there to lead this one big voice. Whatever it is you tell me or what you want to tell me I will listen. Whether it is about fortnite, futbol, math or PE, I will listen. And I will never stop listening and communicating until we have our one big voice heard at ACT. Thank you and vote for Jackson Mailey."

* Day 80 *

I still haven't heard back from AADF on my proposal and it's driving me a bit nuts. My obsessive nature needs something else to distract my brain and thank goodness I have this contract for Manderina to work on. I've been in Albania for five or so weeks and I'm working on two proposals. I'm feeling good and hope one of these or even both of these come through. We will see.

The other thing on my mind is Jackson's speech. He's going to stand in front of the entire 6th grade class to deliver his message. I wish they allowed parents to come watch. He's one of five running and the only boy. 11 years old. Moved to Albania two months ago. Attends a school that is 87% Albanian. 6000 miles away from home. And he has this kind of courage and confidence. Maybe I haven't screwed him up like I thought. I look forward to seeing what this kid does in his future. I'm truly inspired by his adaptability and bravery. I worried about bringing him here. He struggles from anxiety and obsessive behaviors. Gifts his parents bestowed on him. Last school year was a low point for him. He didn't connect with his teacher, "friends" were bullying him, and he spent a lot of time pulled out because he was too advanced for his class. He has a pleaser personality like me, which makes defending oneself a lower priority. Adversity builds character, but his bright and funny spirit was dimming and it was breaking my heart. A few weeks in another country and he wants to lead his fellow students. I did not see that coming.

I pick up the kids from school and Jackson brushes the whole thing off, offering me very few details. Sean called me to let me know the crowd went crazy for him. Someone even chanted, "Jackson, Jackson, Jackson!" On our way home, we stop into our favorite shop, which is a makeshift mini mart in a couple's garage. Herme greets us with smiles and the kids grab snacks and drinks to take to soccer. First soccer game today. My little nuggets are crushing this new life challenge. When Sean and I accepted his job offer to come here, I wrote down how I felt our parenting approach should be. How we parent is extremely personal, but all the clichés are right. It's the hardest and most rewarding job you can take on. These kids are small versions of you in some way. Knowing that, you have the ability to connect with them in ways you respond to best. I think this is the center of the bond. How would you mentor yourself to face this crazy world head on? In a way, it's like a do over. Our children are an evolution of us if we can do enough to guide them to reach for growth sooner than we could. I wrote…

Don't keep me safe.
Don't shield me from what's real,
under the cloak of being my protector.
Instead, show me.
Tell me the stories of conflict, betrayal, judgement, and triumph.
Educate me.
Build me an arc of knowledge that empowers me to weld
the burden of growing up a woman. a man.
Give me the tools to find resolve in myself.
Show me how to love myself or love me hard until I know how.
Respect my abilities to understand the world at a young age.
It will not strip me of my innocence.
It will give me a fighting chance.
One that is needed when sweetness, obedience,
and good looks won't suffice.
Help me practice speaking up when I feel weak.
When my face gets hot and my stomach drops.
Push me.
Get me from nauseated to weight in both my feet.
To lift my chin without flinching.
And the ability to look someone in the eyes
Correct them when they shoot back with, "you're missing the point."
Drive my shoulders back to assert
my understanding of what's being addressed.
Because it's merely their insecurities that led to such a remark.
Why?
Because there will be many.
Many that won't give me the stage.

Won't grant me the courtesy of saying I belong or I'm right.
Who will even knock me down.
Help me navigate the group dynamic of a boardroom.
Set me down a path where I don't shut down
with my shoulders hedging forward
when I am the only woman around the table.
Invite me to these settings early on.
Don't have the boys on the golf course
while the women mind the kitchen.
Wedge me right in there.
Laughing at the bad innuendos and forming a handicap.
Prepare me for the pace.
Don't go easy on me.
To the point that pressure doesn't break me.
Failure is just a learning moment and let me taste victory.
Involve me in group sports.
Force me if I don't want it.
Let me feel how it matters.
The way people count on you and you count on them.
And winning isn't individual.
Let me see the world outside of my home.
I mean really see it.
To get tickled pink about the subtle differences
from place to place, face to face, and taste to taste.
Grab my face and make me notice the sunset and sunrise.
Introduce me to a relationship with Nature.
Don't give me all the answers.
While I respect your experience, it will not be exactly mine.
Instead coach me through problem solving myself.
To trust my instincts
while tempering my maturing emotional intelligence.
Have the patience to taxi me to and sign me up for it all.
I don't know what my passion is yet,
but starting the search early on is good.
I want to find what makes me light up when I talk.
Do you know the answer?

Stop asking me if I like someone at school.
Inquire about my day, interactions, points of interests.
Don't obsess about what I want to be when I grow up
and neither will I.
Help guide me to what makes me happy now.
Show me my path is not set. It is what I make of it.
Break the gender norms in the household.
Where women aren't defined by their child rearing,
clean house, and ability to put a good meal on the table.
Expose me to the division of labor
between a man and a woman
that gives them each the time to laugh,
put their feet up, and sit in solitude.
Don't take this lightly.
You are my guide, my mentor, my mom.
I will trust you before I trust anyone.
I will love you before my first crush. My first kiss.
Don't keep me safe. Don't shield me from what's real.
I've got a long winding life to live and I can use a little advantage.

* Day 81 *

He did it. Jackson won class representative. I can't predict the future, but I'd wager a guess that he'll remember this moment for the rest of his life. He, like most, wants to be chosen by others. It's reaffirming. Builds confidence in who you are. When your life tally is low on moments like these, it's tough to not question yourself. To wonder if there's something wrong with you. I can see happiness run throughout his entire body. I know it won't last forever, but being here and present for Jackson, in this moment, is something I'll always remember. Traveling a lot in the first years of his life, I regret not being there more. Even if we were back in the US and my work didn't require travel, I'd still miss out. By the time I'd usually get home the raw energy of good news has subsided. Picking them up from school every day has been a great gift.

* Day 82 *

Still no word from AADF, but I got approval on my first local contract in Albania. I am responsible for strategic partnerships for DMO Albania, a NGO Manderina Promotions started last year. My first assignment is to consult on the marketing for the 2018 Tirana Photo Festival, develop materials outlining the sponsorship and donor program, design a communication plan, and put it all into action. They are months behind and I have a huge learning curve being new to the city and not being able to speak the language. Seems nearly impossible. I'm told my American accent will work to my advantage. We will see. Not sure if I will land any sponsors, but it could lay a decent foundation for the next event and this position gives me the chance to get myself out there meeting people. If I don't land any sponsors, this whole effort will be pro bono. I'm ok with that. I want to help these women and they need a lot of it. Besides, it's fun to have a little project to work on with a team again. My mood is shifting. The meeting is set for Monday to finalize the contract and get signatures.

* Day 83 *

Saturday is here. Time for another adventure. I've arranged for us to drive
east for about 2.5 hours to a country we have never visited, Macedonia. We'll
be staying in Ohrid for the night and seeing one of the deepest and oldest
lakes in Europe, Lake Ohrid, for the first time. Researching beforehand, I
learned it has a unique aquatic ecosystem. A natural spring from underneath
feeds the lake and it has more than 200 endemic species making it of
worldwide importance. We'll be crossing the border, which means I need to
also arrange for a green card to take the rental car out of the country. 40 euros
for the green card and only 25 euros for the rental itself. Government taxes.
You gotta love 'em. I can only hope that part of the money goes to expanding
and improving these roads.

The terrain is incredibly mountainous, especially as we enter Elbasan County.
The rock is covered with lush evergreens, reminding me of the jungles of
Hawaii and the forests of the Pacific Northwest. Small villages, that take but
a blink of an eye to get through, are weaved in all along the way. It's similar
to our drive to Vlorë in some ways, but we're definitely inland with no sea
bordering us. Once you get on the other side of one mountain, it can open
up and show you vast lands that are yet to be fully developed. Farm lands sit
in the valleys between the mountain ranges and occasionally you see livestock
roaming free. I'm glad we're doing this in daylight. The whole drive is really
scenic. Makes the time go by quickly.

Coming in from the north side, we take a turn and there's Lake Ohrid. It's
just a brief glimpse, but wow. I want to see more. Before we know it, we're at
the border with all our paperwork in hand. Since it's close to noon, there is
quite a line. We heard it could get busy due to Albanians coming to Ohrid
simply to have a nice Saturday lunch. 40-minute wait and then we're on our
way to get more views of this gorgeous body of water. It's like seeing Lake

Tahoe for the first time, but no one is on the water. Completely empty. Can't wait to touch it.

We arrive in Ohrid with great anticipation. The sky is blue and summer heat continues even in late September. Our Airbnb is right on the water. We drop everything and head out to see the lake up close and grab lunch. I didn't imagine the oldest lake being so crystal clear. We can see right to the bottom. Bordering the water is a wide white stone promenade. Perfect for a stroll. Docks extend out and the kids point to the perfect place to jump off the rocks into the water. They'd do it right now if their tummies weren't grumbling for food. The marina area is filled with men with sunbaked leathery skin offering rides in their water taxi. Nice shady spots and blooming flowers, in an adjacent park, slows our pace. All the park benches are full with lounging individuals resting in the heat. The land curves in the distance, giving the area a cove or bay like feeling. Inviting a closer look, the densely-populated curve is full of red clay roof tops. We keep walking and run right into a row of restaurants lining the water with their umbrella shaded tables. Everything looks so clean, new, and high class. All around us people are speaking other languages, but my eyes see a lunch spot that could be in California. We feast on American style cuisine and look out on the water. I scroll through ExploringMacedonia.com on my phone to learn more about the area.

> *Archaeological finds indicate that Ohrid is one of the oldest human settlements in all of Europe. The Lake itself is over three million years old. Ohrid town is first mentioned in Greek documents from 353 B.C, when it was known as Lychnidos or "the city of light." Only much later in 879 A.D, was it renamed Ohrid. The name probably derives from the Macedonian phrase "Vo Hrid" – roughly meaning "the town on the hill."*

Originally, we'd planned on going back to the room, but our curiosity sets us on an exploration of the town. It's the hottest part of the day, nearly 90 degrees, but we drag the kids along. We want to reach a point we see in the distance, but stopping at many places along the way lengthens our stroll. I've never been here, but it all feels reminiscent of places I've been. I'm not sure who designed this waterfront or who architected the homes, but the changing borders of this region are reflected in everything. It lacks its own identity. European for sure, but I can't put my finger on it. Italian, Greek, German, Spanish, French, and even Swiss influences. Old town is cobble stoned like most old towns, but some of the roads are wide enough to drive on. We weave in and out of religious statues and around Byzantine churches. Coming from Albania, all these Christian religious artifacts make me keenly aware of how little there is in our new home city. Water willows line the pebble rock shoreline, white swans have their beaks buried in their feathers taking a nap, and a creaky wood bridge in the water starts to become our path as we make our way toward 13th century St. Jovan Kaneo Church. The high sun casts shadows down on all the stone.

Perched on the edge of the water, as if it dropped from the sky, sits a combination of Byzantine and Armenian architectural styles. The gorgeous church looks down at the water, but you can climb up even further to look down on it. The glints of red brick reflecting in the light. Hot from the sun, we take shade under a tree and sit there for a while. The view can stir anyone's spirit. I could sit here for hours, but the kids are looking at me with red faces and sweaty hair. Time to stop looking at the water. The kids want to get in and they deserve it. Legs fatigued from the two hour walk, we make our way off the hill. Timed like a true salesman, we're approached and wooed onto a water taxi to bring us back. How can we resist? Plus, it's a nice treat to see the church from the water. The water is calm and we all drag our fingers from the sides of the boat to feel the cool.

As soon as we hit land, Sean and the kids are practically sprinting to the Airbnb to get their suits on. Within 15 minutes, the kids locate the pier, run down, and jump in. Little fish follow their every move and kiss at their skin. Nice way to unwind from the day. It's only been a day. We left Tirana this morning, but it feels like forever ago as I lay out on a towel reading. At my eye line Jackson is practicing his dives. Sean is floating out even further to enjoy some solitude. Izzy is climbing all over the rocks dripping water on my book when she stops over me to say hi. Peaceful. I put my toe in the water to see how cold it is, but that's enough for me. They enjoy every ounce of their swim in the freshwater lake as the sun starts to go down. Must get these kids clothed before they freeze. I manage to bribe them out with some promised ice cream while we plant our booties on a bench together to watch the sunset. At the base of the pier, I spot an older man sitting cross legged in his brown capri pants. His bike is behind him and his legs dangling down to the water as he reads his hard bound book. In my mind, I assume he's reading poetry. He is wrapped in pure leisure. A calm comes over the water and Ohrid becomes even more magical as the sun goes down and the outdoor lighting comes on. Ready for an easy-going night, we sit outside for dinner and play cards until the late evening. I love time away with this little family of mine.

* Day 84 *

Morning comes quicker than I'd like. Sun shining through the windows has us up and packing. Time to make the trek back, but first a couple cups of strong coffee and breakfast. The visit was short, but I'm glad we had the chance to meet the charming town of Ohrid. Getting on the road early is a good thing because there are a couple more stops on my list. We've seen the north side of the lake. To get a full picture, we've decided to make our way south around the lake to cross the border at Pogradec.

Another beautiful day for a drive. Windows rolled down to feel the 85-degree day. You can start to see the fall effect on the leaves covering the mountains. We drive past quite a few people attempting to bike around the lake. The water is calm. Like glass. And still no one is on the water. We've only been driving for 20 or so minutes, but I have to get out and look around. The morning haze on the surface creates a mystical look and the water willows have me under a spell. The shades of blue from the sky and the water provide a backdrop that makes the green leaves pop with color. It's out of a storybook. The bend of the trunk leans toward the lake and for a second I can picture a bread, cheese, and wine picnic on a blanket turning into a lazy nap leaning against the tree with a book on my chest. My daydream is interrupted with the fact I'm not alone. Getting a hard stare from the family. Time to continue.

Bend after bend of the road reveals more hidden treasures. We arrive at the archaeological site Bay of Bones. The name references the remains of animals and vessels that still exist under the water between 7-16 feet below the surface. If you're a diver, you can visit the underwater excavation. It's also known as the Museum on Water and it truly is that. According to Lonely Planet,

> *In prehistoric times Lake Ohrid was home to a*
> *settlement of pile dwellers who lived literally on top of*
> *the water, on a platform supported by up to 10,000*

*wooden piles anchored to the lake bed. The remains of
the settlement were discovered at this spot and were
gradually excavated by an underwater team between
1997 and 2005; the museum is an elaborate
reconstruction of the settlement as archaeologists think
it would have looked between 1200 and 600 BC.*

I've been to many historical sites, but this is in my top five. I know it's a re-creation, but it's really well done. Walking around the 21 rectangular houses and three round ones used for rituals, feels transcendent. Each house has different set ups inside with animal hides, beds, and kitchen areas. We pop in and out of each one with wonder. They are made of wooden materials, plaster, and covered with thatching and cattails. The earth tones against the emerald water reminds me of the stilt house photos I've seen of Bali, but standing in Macedonia we're nearly 7000 miles away from there. Simply incredible.

We continue our drive along the water heading toward the Monastery of St. Naum where we will sightsee and have lunch. Still full from breakfast and itching for one last dip in the lake before we head home, we stop at a beach that is empty once again. There is one family having a birthday party, but that's about it. I assume my sunbathing book reading position. Sean and the kids get back in the water. Jackson is having fun with the little fish that follow him to eat the dead skin off his body. They seem to respond to sound, which makes him feel like the king of the sea. His hands are up in the air and it's clear he's lost in his imagination. It's hotter than I expected so I even indulge in a dip. The sucking of the fish is such a strange sensation. It keeps me from staying in the water longer.

The time is ticking on and I know this family under hangry situations. I try to avoid it at all costs. We have a few snacks in the car, but we need to get to our next stop. A quick change out of our suits and we're back on the road.

Arriving at St. Naum couldn't be more different than our tranquil time at the beach. This is THE Macedonia tourist attraction situated only .6 miles from the Albanian border. People dressed in their Sunday best are everywhere. Lunch spots are slammed with piles of plates, with fries, stacked on the countertops waiting for grilled meat to be set on top. A wedding is even being performed on the beach and wild peacocks roam the property like it's no big thing. A bit overwhelmed, we quickly grab the first available table we see and have a mediocre, at best, meal.

Lake Ohrid is supplied by three rivers and the natural spring that bubbles up from underground is on this property. Restaurants sit adjacent to the spring and rowboats line around the perimeter waiting to take you on a tour. It feels like a tourist trap, but we climb onto the boat anyhow because it was recommended as a must see from Erin. At least it takes us away from the noise and bustling pace. Our guide graciously shares his knowledge of the spring. Prespa Lake, on the other side of the Galicica Mountains, sits higher up in elevation and feeds part of its water to Lake Ohrid through underground channels. These fresh water sources are why Lake Ohrid stays so pristine. Researchers say every 70 years the sea water is replaced by fresh water. We reach down to touch the cold water as he continues and once we get away from the crowds it's very tranquil. All I can hear is the water dripping off the wooden oar. The flora, a luscious green above, around and below the water creates an illusion that makes everything seem infinite. It also works as a natural filtering system to preserve the quality of the water. He rows us over the actual bubbling source. Just enough sunlight is coming through the trees to brighten the still clear water. Looking at the white sandy bottom of the lake, your eyes can spot cone piles of sand moving as the natural spring trickles in. Like the earth is breathing. Nature is fascinating.

Getting back to land, we have one more site to see before we head home. We walk uphill to visit a scene that is familiar to the one we experienced in Ohrid. Built along the cliff's edge, the Eastern Orthodox Monastery of St. Naum stands sturdy in its Byzantine style. It's named after the man who founded it and it's said he's even buried in the church. The setting and view of the lake provides a space for contemplation like St. Jovan Kaneo Church, but it's hard to imagine with all the selfies being taken around us. I suppose I've been spoiled by having our other recent destinations mostly to ourselves.

We drive back from Macedonia feeling like we've been gone a lot longer than 29 hours. Travel has a way of making me think differently about time. Nine hours behind a desk or drive to another country and back in the same amount of time? I'll take country hopping please. Thankful for how we spent our time this weekend. What a beautiful trip. We get home late. Grab a couple of cheap pizzas. Eat and then crash. School and work tomorrow.

* Day 85 *

Monday morning run in the sunshine gets my day started. A photo montage of our trip is playing in my mind, but I transition to the realization that I'm working today. After my run, I'll shower up and head into the "office" to finalize my contract with Manderina, get signatures, and share the pitch deck I put together.

Wanting a change, I decide to take a different way to catch a cab. As I get to the taxi queue an older woman swoops in and takes my cab. I guess I snooze I lose. I then notice the rest of the cabs are parked with no one in them. It's around lunch time so people must be on a break. I start to walk to find another queue. It's hot. I'm dressed in heels and a wrap dress. I start to sweat. Trying to find any shady part, I do my best to keep my cool but there are no cabs. What the hell. Restaurants and bars are packed and I need to get to the center of the city. About a 30 min walk to the office, I pull out Google Maps and try to direct myself. This is the first time I've walked this. Many times, in a cab, not paying attention. I get to the end of the street I'm supposed to turn on and try to pick up my pace. Just then I notice that my duration keeps getting longer on Google Maps. I bet my signal is just bad. I keep walking. Finally, it dawns on me. Eight minutes of walking in the wrong direction I realize I turned right instead of left. Shit. I'm going to be cutting it close walking the whole way and I will leave no time to grab a bite before the meeting. I'm even shaking a bit from the low blood sugar. I message to let them know I'm running a few minutes behind. Not an unusual thing for Albanians, but I'm always at least 10 minutes early to anything. I grab a flaky spinach and cheese byrek from a sidewalk counter to put something in my stomach.

Once I get there, I take a minute to fan myself. Wipe the sweat from my nose and forehead. It takes me about 20 minutes into the meeting to cool down, but I do my thing sweat and all. I leave with everything I wanted to accomplish. The terms are approved and the contract is double signed. Feeling good, but now the hard work begins.

* Day 86 *

I put in a full day of work. I'm in a groove. Admitting to myself how my spirit feels more alive today, is difficult to admit. Much of these skills sit in the back of my head and I forget they are there until I call upon them. I draw up a full communication plan, write two sample lead generation emails, research local companies, finalize the pitch deck, advise on the contents of the website, and announce on LinkedIn my new ALIST client DMO Albania. The whole thing is surreal.

We've been invited to a surprise birthday party for Ervisa that Brandt is throwing. I think we'll be the only Americans besides Brandt, but I'm excited to celebrate her and meet her family and friends. We arrive at a restaurant which sits in a large courtyard. Brandt explains that this is the place they held their wedding reception. The space is beautiful. Sitting right in the center is a large, long table, covered with a white linen tablecloth and celebratory decor. It reminds me of the table I sat around with our friends in Oregon a month ago. We spend the evening eating and laughing under the stars. Raised glasses of Raki and champagne, in honor of the birthday girl, continue into the night while the kids play on the swing set. We seem to fit right in. The warm smiles around the table make Tirana feel like home.

Chapter 14

Absolving yourself creates much more room to breathe.

* Day 87 *

Tired from the night before, I muster up the strength to get back to my computer and push through more endless tasks for this new job. Working again has emotions about past careers dredging up. Before I have to get the kids from school, I zone out and watch a few episodes of '*Friends*' on Netflix to offset the mood.

* Day 88 *

Yesterday's funk is still with me. Eva and Alma message me. My new business cards are ready to be picked up. Getting outside of this apartment should help. I manage my morning routine to give myself enough time to walk into the office. The sun is shining, but the Fall crisp air sets the right tone for my walk under the trees along the river. Much better than the jolting horn happy cab drivers. Earbuds in, my mood is easing with each step. The leaves on the trees are starting to match the yellow painted buildings. Deep exhales and I arrive refreshed. It's a quick visit, but worth the trip. Seeing my name on paper with an Albanian nonprofit seems momentous. For years, I've tried to move into the nonprofit sector, but in the US it's tough to crack into. Being an underdeveloped country, Albania is full of them. I guess this is my path. I treat myself to lunch and then walk home feeling accomplished.

* Day 89 *

Today marks two months in Albania. What a tumultuous time. It's had it all. Highs, lows, and everything in between. We drained most of our savings. Finding our footing and establishing a renter in our old home took much more than we expected. Sean and I are still struggling with establishing a life here, but somehow it still feels worth it. I know I am far away in miles, but I also feel so far removed from the US. Only chatter on social media keeps me connected. The news headlines are lined with injustice, hate, another shooting, oppression towards women, and shouting matches of the opposing sides are still as loud as when we left. The negative rhetoric is full of rage. It can make a dark mind sit in "what's the point" land, which reaffirms my reason for wanting this break. I have homesick moments, but I don't want to go back any time soon. It may mean I have to work fulltime sooner than I planned, but that's better than raising my kids in a country that's so hostile and fear driven. Constant polarizing conversations that aren't improving. The country is breaking and it's going to get worse before it gets better. Suicide rates are increasing. Poverty is spreading. Depression and pill popping is on the rise. Addiction is running rampant. I scroll down on my phone and see Dr. Christine Blasey Ford's opening testimony against Brett Kavanaugh. A witch trial of the times. Reminds me of watching the Anita Hill testimony in 1991 from the wheeled in TV at my middle school. Both women's conviction and strength is admirable. The quiver in Ford's voice has me in tears. Solidarity. I've been there Dr. Ford. Not on display in front of the entire world to see, but I stand with you. Sadly, not much has changed since 1991.

The carousel of American news is churning strong since Trump took office, but Albania's love affair with America still remains. On October 3, 2018, the

Diversity Green Card Lottery Program, commonly referred to as "the golden ticket," opened for application submission and closes November 6, 2018. It's the same day as our midterm elections. Every year one hundred thousand Albanians try their chances at what they believe is a better life and an opportunity to live the American Dream. With Trump in office, there are talks of this program getting canceled, which would make this possibly the last year for applications after being established 30 years ago.

To be honest, I didn't know anything about the program until I left the US and moved to Tirana. When Albanians hear my American accent, they are shocked. It's not very common around here. When they learn that I choose to live here and I'm not on vacation, they immediately ask, "Why?" And I don't know where to begin in my answer.

The Diversity Immigrant Visa program was established under the US Immigration Act of 1990 and gives the winners and their families the chance of permanent residency in the US. Every year the US State Department allocates 50,000 permanent resident visas in an attempt to diversify the US with immigrants from these countries. The next few weeks is a collection of applicants for the random drawing being performed to elect 2020 winners.

For someone in my situation, it gives me a lot to think about. My Filipino grandparents immigrated for the same reasons. A better life. Land of opportunity. The American Dream. Yet, here I am living outside of my country for several reasons I simply cannot share with my Albanian friends. America is revered. It sits upon the highest pedestal even with Trump in office. Anything I could say wouldn't change their perception or desire to go there. Regardless of who I am, my citizenship puts me at a higher station in the world and some think in a higher place in life. It's the first time I find people more focused on my citizenship than the brown color of my skin or that I am a woman. To them, I am privileged. That thought is a challenge to process.

I know most of the Albanian population wants to leave, but I see beauty here. In the people and the surroundings. I see a country of unrealized opportunity. I see rich historical traditions woven into daily life and not yet forgotten. I see pristine landscapes untouched by commercialism. I see farm to table that isn't a trend, but a way of life. I see ancient relics still standing after thousands of years just waiting to be honored. I see the simplicity of living as a community. Connected not digitally, but physically and honoring the value of face-to-face time. I see the warmth and acceptance of outsiders. I see physical touch and public affection embraced between men and women. I see family friendly, bright and colorful environments with each turn. I see how I am charmed by the relaxed pace. In Albania, I see a better quality of life for me and my family and I am forever grateful for being here. In life, we can't always see the beauty in things. We need someone else to see it. For the beauty to rise above the ugly. Because the ugly sticks out more in the mind. But do I see all of this just because I'm a foreigner? With grass being greener? I don't know, but does it matter? What matters is how I feel. Now. How this place has had a hand in that evolution. Plus my American status works to my favor here too. I'm not sure my country would afford the lottery winners with the same treatment, but filled with hope year-after-year they apply.

I suppose the lesson for me is perspective. It's very important. We all have things we long for and that drives the heart and mind. We see what we want to see. It can be a challenge to find the positives in our immediate situation. To even lose pride in your own country. To the point, we feel the need to escape. I see much of that here and I surely see it back in the States. Both countries have their ugly sides. I suppose I've realized my American Dream is that I have the freedom to come and go. To choose. To experience where and when I please. It is a gift my grandparents gave me and I am forever in service of being deserving of it. It is one of the many reasons I hope this program stays open. We all deserve the choice to seek a better life, whatever that means and wherever we want our journey to take us.

* Day 90 *

Starting a home somewhere else can leave you stripped of patterns that once provided you comfort. All the things that made bad days bearable. A codependent relationship I wasn't aware of until now. Like quickly reaching for the wine or liquor to pour into the pretty glasses I owned. Opening the bottle. The smell. The sound of it pouring. The color reflecting light in the glass. The weighted feel of it in my hand that somehow evened me out as I swirled it. Sipping while simultaneously exhaling. Almost as if I couldn't do so without it.

Portland is rich in many things - liquor, beer, wine, drugs, food, entertainment, shopping, arts, nature – that helped me layer the buried events and move forward. Sweet escapism. Nearby, I had friends that knew me. The go to faces and stories that make me laugh till I peed. The ones that know when to hug me or to just listen or to dance with me in my kitchen. The best evening highs to distract a girl like me. Night turns to dawn and the new day grabs me in the gut. Time to face what I pushed aside. Because life isn't easy. You can change the location, but hard will find you.

If I separate the idea of "home" from these dependencies, I tend to draw conclusions that it's not home that I miss. When life is good, when my center is there, my dependency is less. But when I have a crappy day, I can't put my learned behaviors in motion because my new home doesn't offer what Portland does. It's an achy feeling because there's nothing to mask the sad. Cope. Vulnerability can suck and we rarely have time to face it.

We are products of our environment. The worlds we build all around us to tick the seconds, minutes, hours, days, weeks, months, years of our lifetime. Maybe that's why people say Portland is the place where young people come to retire. While it's a great city, it can cast a haze over your eyes, numbing what you let it numb and filling voids you aren't ready to fill another way.

Stepping away, even for a little while, and being alone in this apartment all day, without my co dependencies, has been a sobering experience. A sort of detoxing. The first 60 days were rough, I'm not gonna lie, but now I feel like I am seeing clearer. Lighter. I'm facing what scares the hell out of me. Taking risks. Challenging traditions. Living the adventure instead of longing for it. Building better relationships. Seeing more of my husband, my kids, the world. And I have no idea what the future holds. It's not a forever state of mind, but nonetheless it's a vantage point I'm thankful for achieving.

When I go home to visit next month, I won't be detoxing. For me, the holidays are for indulging in family, friends, food, and drink. But this time it won't be to mask the sad. My heart and mind are healthier. My "vices" are purely for fun and celebration. I'm bringing a genuine smile and hugs for all who want them. I still have work to do, but I'm on that path of living a life where no one owns my happiness, but me.

* Day 91 *

The fight over finances with Sean continues. I'm still seeing the positive, but he thinks we are in over our heads and should go home. There is a real possibility in making this work, but it's highly variable. We have dependencies and some of them are out of our control. I want to stick it out as long as we can. I still haven't fully conveyed to Sean why I need this so much. His knee jerk reaction to head home at Christmas isn't personal to me. It's actually logical, but each time he suggests the departure I feel like it's masquerading as a hindrance in giving me what I want. So I lash out. Say things I don't mean. I just need more time. Many more months to get me right. We've come this far and my days in this little apartment are peeling back the yuck. I need to tell him, but I don't know how.

The truth is I've struggled with depression since I was a young child. I had suicidal thoughts as a teenager and even as recently as when I lived part-time in Seattle. Ending everything felt easy. The hole I dug felt too deep to get out. I was living a life that felt all wrong. I didn't want to do it anymore. My job demands created a lifestyle of minimally seeing Sean and the kids. I thought, I'm hardly around anyway so it shouldn't take long to get used to me being gone. I've never shared these feelings with anyone. Writing it down now puts a nervousness in my belly.

My parents divorced when I was five years old. Having a single mom and being the oldest girl of a large family meant taking care of others at an early age. In a lot of ways I was a mother figure before I was a woman. My disengaged father put me on a search for love early on. Taking care of the men in my life and the affection I'd get in return, defined a relationship construct that stunted my "find yourself" phase. As a pleaser, I'd take on multiple personalities. A chameleon. Lacking true moments of self, can have you questioning who you are. Even stealing other identities to blend in or acting in ways unlike yourself. Fake it till you figure it out. In my career, I walked away from trying to be an artist. I surrounded myself with creatives, but I supported their success. Helped them be better. Way easier than helping myself. As a mom and wife, it was no different. This is my crossroads. I must stop making my happiness reliant on being needed. It creates an unhealthy dependency on others to feel purposeful. The cycle puts the balance of give and take off kilter. I see that now. Learning how to care for myself, even though this is all new territory for me, is important. It isn't selfish to be the center of attention.

The yelling continues with Sean, but my mind is elsewhere. Years of past moments flashing. Everything is sitting on the surface. The pain. The heartbreak. The disappointment. The abuse. The secrets. The betrayal. The regrets. The loneliness. The resentment. The loss. How I ran hard from it all. Threw myself in a demanding career and never looked back. And now I'm facing it. Time to purge.

For the past few months, I've dedicated my time and energy to writing again. It's a lot of me sitting inside my head trying to express what I'm feeling. It's raw. Invasive. Draining. I've always thought of myself as a creative individual, but not as a 9-5 profession. Sitting in my apartment every day until 3pm, I'm cocooned. Like personal therapy sessions with myself. As I walk to pick up my kids from school, I try to shake off the emotions of my day and start new. Like 3pm is morning and it's time to be a mom, a wife. Some days are more challenging than others, but I am what I am. A ticking time bomb ready to set off because I didn't shove down my feelings far enough before interacting with others. Thankfully my family forgives me if this happens, but I see how this dedication is changing me. It's heavy and I have incredible appreciation for the artists that keep going. Living in the highly creative space to express an internal state, and then switch to life mode is challenging. We are emotional creatures. Artists spend intense energy exposing themselves, being vulnerable, to complete strangers, and then wait for acceptance or understanding. It takes courage and confidence.

Growing up as a dancer and writer made me a volatile little human. Turning to my business side in my adulthood felt safer, easier to monetize, more controllable, but not as fulfilling. Dedicating time to creativity again has me feeling more like me, but it's unlocking ache I've held onto. I didn't know what would come of journaling daily. I just knew I needed to write down what I was going through. And in turn, it is helping me process other parts of my life. I'm doing my best to wrangle the ugly heads that want to rear themselves. Something I didn't consider when I set out to write every day. I guess that's why when an artist stands up and receives an accolade, he or she thanks the family and friends that stuck by them through it all. We can be assholes.

Sean's face now looks defeated. Lost. But I'm finally standing firm in both my feet. It's time. If I let my sad stories own my life, I will miss out on a lot. I put this process on hold long enough. Sean is struggling with me, but I feel like we're finally getting somewhere. Fear of disappointing or inconveniencing him, hell...everyone, has held me back. It has eroded my inner happiness. I don't know if it's my upbringing or just my DNA or maybe a little of both, but it's a quality that pervades both my personal and professional life. I'm trying to find balance in this phobia along with defining what makes me happy; doing something that derives no value from pleasing someone else. The master of yourself. It is out of my nature, but discovery that is born out of this choice is extremely fulfilling. Owning your own happiness is freeing.

Helping others, not at the expense of me, mixed with learning something new fills my spirit. Quiet moments of observation to ignite creative expression makes me whole. Then loving hard on my family and closest friends grounds me in stability. I need my life to be filled with all three of these things. I couldn't define it till now. It was like I was allergic to something and to find out what it was I had to take everything away. Only to reintroduce things back slowly. This experience is life changing. We are nowhere near financial bankruptcy. We've piled up retirement money. We still own the house. We will get through this. I'm stretching. I'm honoring who I am. I know who I am. We will come back even stronger than when we left. I am certain of it.

* Day 92 *

Pretty relaxing Sunday. In an attempt to continue to assimilate and find joy in the little things, I've started a new tradition. Seek out different breakfast or brunch spots and walk in the sunshine to get there. It gets us exploring the city and I love breakfast foods. Walking the streets, we search for new murals to add to our memory banks. There is new construction in Tirana, but many of the old boxy communist buildings remain. And because land grab was a free-for-all after communism fell, the urban planning is lacking. Construction happened piecemeal as money became available. This is still the approach. Plus, you are taxed less if you are still in progress. Traveling the country, you can see many buildings unfinished. In Tirana, high rises are bunched and scattered without much of a grid. Navigating is a challenge. Visiting someone's home for the first time requires a lot of verbal explanation because the entrance isn't obvious. Having an address isn't enough. Landmark directions are a necessity, which is fine by me, but drives Sean nuts.

When Edi Rama, a former art professor, became mayor in 2000, he didn't necessarily repair the infrastructure. Being the poorest country in Europe, there wasn't any money. Leaning on his background, he started a painting campaign to fill the drab facades with vibrant bold colors drawn in abstract patterns and shapes. This was at a time when people needed everything (running water, electricity, roads, food, jobs, etc.) but I wonder what it was like to look up or out and see this new view. Many neighborhoods and villages today still need these essential things so I've heard mixed reviews from Albanians about this approach, this distraction. You can paint the walls, but the work still needs to be done. You can't hide it.

In 2013, Rama became Albania's prime minister leading the socialist party. In 2015, the government employed Franko Dine, a 24-year-old from Vlorë, to continue his mural graffiti to cover key buildings. His talents brightened my mood today. When the architecture is pre, during, and post communism design mixed with the colorful paint, it creates an eclectic personality. It feels uniquely Albanian. You may be poor, but at least dress up like you're not.

Chapter 15

Beauty can be found between the tension of dark and light.

* Day 93 *

New week. Another morning run, but that's as much effort as I want to put in this day. I have to say it's kinda nice to not face a day you aren't ready to face. There have been countless times I was feeling melancholy and I had to still do, albeit fake, the happy song and dance. Even won some new business at work or led a team in a creative brainstorm when I was in the trenches of the lull. Life typically doesn't have a pause button when you're feeling low.

I've also enjoyed very little dressing up these last few months. Living primarily in sweats when it's cold and linen shorts when I'm hot along with a messy bun and no makeup has become a signature look that matches my relaxed state. No tummy and thigh control tights sucking it all in. No buttons to button. No heels to balance on. No hair straightening. All natural. Letting my wild curly hair do what it will in this humidity. Lazy. My only responsibilities today are getting the laundry and dishes done. It can be a good and a bad thing. Placing yourself in situations you have to fake happiness can actually lead to real positive moments. Sulking alone can perpetuate the dark cloud a bit longer. My solitude bubble will burst when the kids get out of school. For now, I'm going to enjoy this freshly picked white pomegranate from a tree in our courtyard. Pulling out all the seeds and feasting in the sunshine on the balcony has become one of my favorite ways to pass the time. Not sure what I'm going to do in the winter, but everything is brighter when paired with this wonderful sun. Just have to get out in it. Fall is beautiful.

* Day 94 *

Alright. I need to push myself to socialize. My introverted tendencies are having a field day with my emotions. After a quick meeting about the Photo Festival, I meet up with my friend Erin for lunch. A girl from Wyoming, living in Albania after serving in the Peace Corps, who speaks the language and has been married to an Albanian for the past year is like a plotline for a television series. She's 10 years younger than me and I find her perspective on the world fascinating. She hasn't been home for a while and I am loathing the US while being a bit homesick. This should be fun. We split a bottle of wine and hit multiple topics on the rooftop of a local restaurant.

Erin has been living in a world where women are still being sold into marriages at a very young age. Where opportunity is a man, and women's rights are pretty nonexistent or rarely discussed publicly. Abuse is a cultural norm and sex trafficking is a reality in the smaller villages. Across the table, I'm the female corporate junkie who left the game; tired of the misogynist and abusive environments that only let me climb so high. I did well for myself financially, but making six figures in my 20s came at a price. My struggle feels trite compared to what Erin tells me, but my pain is real to me.

I left my country physically and mentally burned out. A country built on hope had me at my most hopeless. I was much too close to the thumb I was under to see what was happening in the world around me. The election of Trump unearthed a pain that was deep. I knew racism was everywhere, but the white supremacy rhetoric was all so public. People all around me were wearing safety pins and I didn't know how to respond. Feelings were justified, but positive perspective was hard to find. It wasn't healthy and I couldn't talk about it with anyone. Stepping away, even for only a few months, and watching it from afar has me on my way to finding resolve. To maybe return to the US once again someday without the jadedness and fear.

I try to explain to Erin where I am in my life, but I know it isn't easy for her to see from her vantage point. I come from a place of privilege as an American. Albania, although surrounded in natural beauty, still has the shroud of communism over its eyes. The sexist culture, human and drug trafficking, oppressive policies, and corruption bred through poverty create a world where patriotic pride is practically gone. Even more so than what I have left in my heart for America. Justice isn't even a thing. There is no fair. Living in it is exhausting and Erin wants to go home but the Visa process for her husband is awful. She is stuck. Hearing from Erin what America does offer, instead of focusing on what it doesn't, starts to open my eyes.

As a brown-skinned mixed race woman, I used to roll my eyes at the melting pot metaphor when describing our country, but it really is. Sure the 1%, heads of corporations and our government are lacking in diversity, but we're now talking about that as a success hindrance. Not just because we want equality, but because the world isn't one dimensional, and it's just plain wrong. There are 327 million people in the United States today. A little over 4% of the world's population. We have Native Americans, Asian Americans, Mexican Americans, African Americans, Latin Americans, etc. The list is endless. We're a microcosm of the world population under the same roof trying to achieve the best way of life possible. The ultimate mixed family with all varying backgrounds and this creates tension in the family dynamics. Dysfunction comes to the surface. Especially because no one really teaches all of us, at the same time and in the same way, how to communicate with one another. We are simply bound together left to figure it out. Work through the oppression our country was founded on, break down the systems that continue to oppress and pull up and out of fear that keeps us wielding guns and divided by party lines.

Inversely, I now live in a country with less than 3 million and mostly of the same background. And I don't just mean the way someone looks. From upbringing, to education, to wealth, to skill sets, to diet, to beliefs, much of the population comes from the same beginning. This is especially attributed to living in isolation during the four decades of communism between 1946 and 1992. And even today there aren't a lot of outside influences on the ground. Tourism is low and not being a part of the EU keeps big businesses away. Many Albanians are discouraged by the progress in the last 30 years, leading to more Albanians living outside of the country than remain. By some definitions, isolation continues here because they are truly void of diversity and firsthand experience with environments encouraging differing perspectives. As someone who loves to study human behavior, living here makes me fear our division even more. We need each other. The middle working class is dying off. Poverty will continue to break down families and communities.

The mixed family fabric in the US would be our greatest strength if we could harness it instead of fear it and takes sides. Families of the same background, have their own struggles, but uniting through what divides us makes our connection even more powerful. It's not easy and we're a young country in relation to the rest of the world. Babies in fact. Only 242 years old if you cite our beginning as the signing of the Declaration of Independence and the US Constitution in 1776. I mean, countries around the world have pubs older than that. Slavery ended only 153 years ago with the ratification of the Thirteenth Amendment in 1865. The vote was granted to women only 98 years ago when the 19th amendment was ratified in 1920. Our first POC president was elected 10 years ago when Barack Obama won in 2008. Same sex marriages were legalized in all 50 states just three years ago with the US Supreme Court's decision on June 26, 2015. Hillary Clinton's 2016 campaign brought the first woman running for a major party and she almost became the President of the United States. We have quite a historical timeline in such a short period of time. And many other countries are still behind what we've achieved.

Our growing pains are inevitable. We all want to see progress, by our own personal definition, and in our lifetime. It may not all happen on our terms, but that doesn't mean our country isn't on an upward trajectory. And when you do get to experience a win for progress in your lifetime, you want more. Because the next milestone feels more attainable. We're hungry for it. It's a fuel for our fire. On top of that, we have a platform to speak out. We can denounce our president if we want. We can leave the country and come back whenever we want. We can run for office if we don't like the current policy.

There are some checks and balances even though it's not perfect. I was raised and encouraged that these were my rights. Rights not equal in the world.

The past two years makes many of us feel like we're going backwards. We are not. We are coming out of closets, dark corners, and from under bed sheets. Whispered conversations are now done so with raised voices for all to hear. Our ugly truths are on the biggest stage and it's a spectacle. We're getting it all out on the table. I'm no therapist, but this my fellow American citizens is progress. Tension breeds reform. This white, man-made, global powerhouse of a capitalist country was not born without sacrifice. Each of us have our own story on how it has affected our lives and we're finally telling it and people are starting to listen. Good or bad. Diplomacy has kept these truths quiet, swept under the rug, dismissed. Unable to see where we're broken. This is where the real work begins. I couldn't see that a few months ago, but I see that now.

Whenever I argue with my husband and my kids hear us, I tell them that arguing is good in a relationship. It means we care. Even though I need to turn away sometimes, I don't ever want us to grow silent because we have polarizing opinions. Our extremes offer the best place to study and learn because they all have a starting point. Apathy is a killer.

My mom has taught me a lot over the years, but the one thing that I continually return to is empathy. Even if you can't quite figure out why things are the way they are, keep searching. Keep trying to understand. And if empathy isn't there yet, seek to find the good. I now think I'm on that path.

* Day 95 *

Another day home alone and the conversation with Erin is still lingering. Time to yoyo. Did I just make a huge mistake leaving my career? The thought has me spinning. I'm filling my time with a bunch of nonsense. Why spend all kinds of time crafting a LinkedIn post for a few people to read and disregard? Same with my Influence blog. It's all just tiny distractions. To feel like I'm doing something "professional" still. Not ready to let go because work is a part of who I am. Plus I think it's me trying to stay connected, even in an artificial way, so I don't evaporate. Become forgotten. Because once I figure out how to make work a healthy part of me, I will be back.

Scrolling mindlessly I stumble on Brand Week coverage. I see this woman who kind of looks like me, probably five or so years younger, sitting on a stage at Brand Week talking about her successful company. This isn't her first featured speaker moment. TedX and all the rest. In 2015, named by Forbes 30 Under 30 list for Marketing & Advertising. And it hits. I want to be her, but will I ever be? Jealousy compiled with fear and the realization of "what the hell am I doing in Albania" settles in. The kids are thriving in an international private school. Sean is promoted and resumé building. And for the first time, I'm doing nothing for my career. I may be working on me, but I'll never be on 30 under 30 of anything and turning 40 in April means no 40 under 40 chance either. Not sure why this matters, but it does. Stupid. Time to spiral down. Thinking about all the things I'm not. Wondering if I'll ever hold a CEO seat in a successful company before I leave this earth. But will it matter? Is that what I really want? I was doing so good here. Am I pining because it's not mine anymore? Wanting what I cannot have? Disappointed because what I did do wasn't enough for the recognition? Green with envy of someone else's youth and success? There's that word. Success. What is success?

Walking to pick up the kids from school I have a mini meltdown. What if this was all a big mistake? My moment in life, I fail. I take a leap of faith and go splat. On the bright side, I am living in a beautiful place to fail. There is a lot of good coming from this adventure. I have accomplished so much in 40 years and hopefully I have more than 40 more ahead of me. Yes, I can make an impact, but what if I'm more selfish than I think. I don't like the whole "what if" game, but I'm afraid of the regrets. It's just three years off the grid. I should be able to bounce back, right? Shit, I just don't know. Women are actually getting promoted now. Every day it seems another woman is getting promoted on LinkedIn. What if I left the scene at the opportune time for my career? I thought this was what I wanted, but right now I'm not sure. I need to stop talking to the air. Making posts in the social space makes me feel empty. And I pathetically obsess about whether anyone saw, liked, or commented. Writing in this "book" isn't any better. Will anyone ever read this thing? I gotta keep my shit together. I know I'm meant to be here. I am happiest when my mind and heart have space to create and love those around me. But I can't deny the thrill I get from a work high. I need a solution that provides me both or this mini meltdown can be something much bigger. The problem is I don't know where to begin. Agency life is all I've ever known. My own consultancy may be the answer now, but what about long term? How do I attract a team position if I've been individually contributing for years? How do I transition into something else? And here I thought I didn't need corporate life to be happy. I feel side swiped. Knocked off my game. I'm back yearning for senior status. Oy.

* Day 96 *

New day. I got my first bite on a potential sponsor for the Photo Festival. Felt good getting out and pitching again. I think I hooked at least one interested party and that was my goal. I was feeling happy and then the results of the Kavanaugh hearings were announced. How is he not only off the hook, but now he is going to be sitting on our Supreme Court? Men do this because they can. Just do it.

Although I have found some peace out here, I realize I have a lot of anger. That I needed to do the extreme of packing up my family and moving out of the country because I felt driven into a corner. Thousands of microaggressions flood forward into view. They add up. My brain was too tired to confront every instance the color of my skin made me feel less than. My gender the target of harassment. My tireless efforts not being enough. The negativity can be paralyzing. The recent hearings surfaced a lot too. I realize we are more progressive than Albania, but these aren't countries to compare. We are the leaders of the free world and yet there is little protection for women. Especially sexual or physical harassment and abuse. The racism, sexism, treating women as property, the constant pro-life laws hanging in the balance, and rape culture is a big White House parade. And we women, LGBT, POC are supposed to get pumped up and fight this. To rise up in an environment where people felt they actually had to wear safety pins to show we have allies. Again, we are the victims and we have to clean up the shit to not feel like victims anymore. Get organized. Assert our feminism. The battle that will never be fair until these men get even older and die off. Still, we must use OUR "one life" to make an impact because the littlest of ripple makes a big wave. Especially for the little girls today. My little girl included. I know. I shouldn't be so self-serving and walk away. But this is why women, older women, who see stuff, get hard. And I don't want to get hard. I gave it a go for 39 years and I need a break. I want to live my life without the weight.

America is built on this idea of hope. Hope is a tough pill to swallow. It's marketed to us since birth. We can do and be anything we set our minds to if we put in the work. Then you become an adult covered in the slime of childhood and have yet another birth. You realize it's not that easy. So now what? You feel lied to. Or like a failure because others seemed to work hard and got theirs. Or you do things you aren't proud of to get ahead. Or you just get angry and give up. All created equal, my ass.

Being brown and a woman in corporate America felt pretty bottom rung. It was daunting. The hardest worker with the highest profit margins and business growth, but performance reviews cite my tenacity as a hindrance. I'm intimidating. Need to be more likeable. Not VP material. With goals surpassed, I'm left wondering whether outcomes would be different if I was a man or had my mother's skin. And when I get the chance to sit across from the global head of HR, who happens to be a female POC, she talks about how pretty I am and admires my youthful face. A face that can't possibly have the experience to hold a higher title. She spends the whole meeting asking me about eye creams I must use leaving zero time to discuss my contributions as an executive leader.

In my experience, it's grueling work gaining the courage to be heard around a table of all (mostly white) men. But I did it daily. I'm thankful for my allies. Men have such a learned behavior they don't even know their lack of inclusiveness. The bias runs deep. And then those who do know better take full advantage and it's even worse. The corporate structures and processes in place are designed for men by men. Women like me (we ladies badged with "potential") are sent to mentorship programs to learn how to get ahead in the man's world and meanwhile men aren't shipped off to a workshop to learn how to create an environment for women to succeed. It's on the woman to figure it out aka "lean in" and when there are only a few top positions open this environment makes women turn on women. It isn't pretty. Sure, you see a newly appointed woman as CEO or some senior position and fair wage being met in a few places plastered in the headlines, but those women also step down after a year or two. And more women are leaving the workforce every year. Because those promotions were quick fixes. Band-Aids. Fortune published an article about it in May 2018. Promotion, while a problem, isn't the root cause of what's going on here. "While women were at the helm of **6.4 percent** of the companies on 2017's list, that number is now down to 4.8 percent. The biggest reason for this drop, according to Fortune, is that more than a third of Fortune 500 female CEOs resigned in the past year." I like to think they are going to start their own companies. We need systemic changes that move women up the ladder when it's time, not just when she asks for it or as a PR stunt. We must fix the wage and promotion set back women deal with every time they have a child. And please o please end the boys club climate and stop hiring the sexual harassers that were asked to leave other companies. The bad cycles must end.

We are a young country in relation to the rest of the world. I really see that from here. And these older countries still don't have it figured out. The inequality is vast and accepted just about everywhere. As someone who's been up against this for many years, I've decided I won't let my struggles define me. I am on to accepting them because I have to. Not letting them go wouldn't be good for my mental health, so I guess I, too, have stepped down for awhile. Instead, I work on positivity and mentorship with other women, but that doesn't give me much room to share my own angst in all this. Shaking off this negative stance is going to take time, but doing it from afar, putting distance between me and the corporate environment, is improving things. But the hearings are loud and in my face today, as I'm sure is the case for many women around the world. I wonder how they are getting through their day, their month. Are any ladies in the workforce at their most productive these days?

Chapter 16

The door is open. Walking through is up to you.

* Day 97 *

Whoa. Day 96. Feeling rosy and then BAM—confronted by demons. I suppose we all need those days. Today is a new one. I start my morning off with a fun call from my friend Amber. It's her Thursday evening and drinking hour and I'm getting the day started in the Albanian time zone. We laughed for about an hour and somehow a video chat made things right in the world. I needed her and she said the same about me. More good news. Finally heard back from AADF. I won the workshop facilitation project. I cannot believe it. They are flying me to Florence, Italy and paying me enough money to cover the cost of bringing my family for a week long Italian vacation. We're going to explore Florence for the first time, drive to Cinque Terra to show the kids one of our favorite spots, and even squeeze in the leaning tower of Pisa before we fly out. I'm in total shock. An opportunity I wouldn't have if we hadn't come here. A chance I would have missed out on if I hadn't stepped out of this apartment to make connections with others. Cascading decisions have me leading a workshop in a beautiful villa in the middle of Italy's renowned wine country. You just never know where life can take you. Last bit of good news. We got a signed lease from another renter to replace the one who didn't work out with Joan. And we're getting more money from her. It's amazing what a night's sleep can do. The world is right side up again.

* Day 98 *

It's Saturday and Brett Kavanaugh's confirmation to the Supreme Court is happening back in the US. The best way to deal with this is to turn it off and go see something beautiful in the world. With Erin's recommendation, we hike out to Cape of Rodon with her, her husband Behar, Brandt, Ervisa and some of their family and friends. More jaw dropping beauty. We showed a few Albanians this place for the first time. They've never been here and it's so close to Tirana. Now that was an interesting realization. I love influencing others to get out and see the world. Not in an arrogant way, but in feeling like you made someone smile today but mother nature did most of the work. The coast is lined with sand cliffs that have been etched away by the sea. The kids spot faces and objects in sand with pure fascination. It's like staring up at the clouds.

In all our exploring, I continue to gravitate to the many windows and doorways that open up to magical settings. My phone is full of pictures. The castle on the tip of the cape has many that give way to the views of the blue sea. They were probably once used to spot invaders and house cannons and guns. Today, they're natural picture frames for all of us to indulge in. Staring through them makes me reflect. My emotions of my past were trapped and cornered. Perhaps the walls were there on purpose. I wasn't ready to see it. The symbolism of me now going through to the other side has me transforming and absolving a few heavy burdens. Sometimes things don't move as fast as you'd like. It's either not supposed to or you're going the wrong direction. I am here for a reason. I am sure of it. Everything I have done in my life has brought me to this point. Life lesson noted.

* Day 99 *

Our Sunday morning tradition of trying new breakfast places continues. Although I want to stay in bed all day, we try a wannabe New York style bagel place. On our way, we run into a half marathon and a 10K in progress. An annual event that started in 2016. The running community is out and about and it's a sight to see. Another thing to make this feel like home. We even see and shout at Shannon's husband Bobby who we spot in the crowd. Of course, the streets are blocked off so it takes a bit to get to the breakfast spot, but it's another beautiful fall morning and I don't mind the walk. We make it and the bagel is not quite right, but it will do. We then walk all over Tirana seeing even more for the first time. I love exploring this little city. I take Sean and the kids to Pazari i Ri, a new bazaar that recently opened. It was completely renovated as an AADF project and it's reminiscent of the Seattle Pike Place market we are accustomed to in the PNW. Really beautiful space. Vibrant colors, once again, adorn the buildings and it's buzzing. People enjoying the restaurant scene. Farmers, bakers, fishermen, all selling their goods. It's a true market space. We spot pumpkins for our Halloween carving tradition. They aren't cheap and we aren't equipped to take them home today, but knowing they are there brings me excitement. Hope we can find them again when we come back to buy them in a week or two.

We next wander into a mall we haven't been to yet. It's huge with scenic views of Dajti mountains from this glass covered building. We're on the lookout for Halloween costumes, but no such luck. We spot a mattress store. The little sleep I'm getting on our hard bed at the apartment pushes us to try some out. Not incredibly pricey and it feels good allowing the give of a foam mattress to contour my body. I want to bring it home immediately, but we need time to save up. We will be back. We hop in the cab heading back to our side of town, but we have one more stop in us before heading home. Bingo! We found costumes. I heard that Albanians don't know the funny dress up side of Halloween but they get the scary part. So all the costumes are a bit frightening, but the kids are old enough to give it a try. We find something that we can all fit in. It's not the scariest thing there, but we're skeletons and I love it. The Mailey Halloween tradition of family themed costumes will live on.

* Day 100 *

It's a new week, but I'm starting this morning out slow. Yesterday, I suffered from a migraine in the late afternoon. Thunderstorms do that to me and it was loud and active all night. I still have residual this morning, which is why I skipped my Monday morning run. I have a lot to get done to prepare for Italy next week, but today I need to write.

I have all these thoughts going through my head around this life we're now living and my observations the past 100 days. I see now that I needed this departure from the US to shock my system. Wake it up. Stop the runaway train that has gotten so far away from me. You just get going down a path and very rarely stray from it unless there is a big life event. This has been mine. Ours.

As creatures of habit and survival, we tend to collect in our minds what brings us comfort and build bubbles around ourselves to make us feel safe. But we can outgrow these bubbles as the world evolves and we age. Living in this distant land from my hometown, I've nested here. I've relearned what I like and appreciate because I naturally seek it out. I know what makes me feel whole and what weighs me down. Albania has made those things, and me, shine again. We deserve time spent to reassess. This new alignment breeds creativity and opens new windows in the psyche. A self-awareness to move forward with these teachings to live a more joyful life.

I've thought a lot about the phrase "settle down." I've heard this said to me and to others my entire life. As though there is a point in time where we must get the stable desk job, get married, have a mortgage, take on car payments, have two kids and a dog, and just be. Some career choices keep you even more stationary too. No travel involved at all. Punch in and punch out at the same place every day. For some, that is enough, but not me.

Breaks from this worker bee lifestyle are too small and it all depends how much vacation time this stable job or jobs give you. If it's the standard two weeks, you must break it up and share it with family visits and perhaps the occasional weekend getaway. But even if you get five weeks, like we did in the US, the most you can stay in a new place is typically two weeks and even then you've barely scratched the surface of really knowing a place or the people or the culture to truly affect your life views. With 2-3 days to use a year, why not go to an all-inclusive resort to be waited on, surrounded by people who want the same, and veg out in this alternate reality to escape? Then you've really seen nothing but the umbrella above your head and in your drink before you're "rested" and back to the grind to save enough to go back and do it again.

Between being a taxi to and from the scheduled activities and heading into a man-made building to stare into space as you pay to get "exercise," I have to think there must be more. Searching for other goals that pushed me, or to simply break up the monotony, I fell into the running phenomenon. I trained and completed a half marathon. I ran more than a handful of 200 mile relays with friends. But even that started to get too predictable. What else was there?

I've always had these thoughts. I never understood it and of course guilt always creeped in. Was I selfish? Words like 'restless' have negative meaning in this society. Why couldn't I just settle?

It hit the hardest after I had my second kid. Wait. You're telling me you're just supposed to do this over and over again, under the label of tradition, and wait for them to go to college? And my biggest accomplishment in life is being a great mom and wife who raises wonderful kids. And then I become a grandma and help raise my kids' kids. But what if I want more? Am I being too cynical? Is turning 40 this year serving up midlife crisis on a platter?

I am very analytical so trust me when I say I have really thought about this. Especially when I'm suffering from insomnia. Maybe I shouldn't give a toast at a wedding or baby shower anytime soon, but hear me out. We only had two kids and spaced them out by four years. That means we will [get to] do this for 22ish years before we do something else. Something else that might make us happier, healthier, better parents, better people. We must wait till they go to college, if they go to college, for our next chapter to begin. And these are the times of our life. The best life. Maybe I've been in marketing too long, but I'm not buying it.

I get why my parent's generation may think this. They are the kids of a different time. The Great Depression era or being first generation in the US might have weighed in the back of their minds as they make their less risky life decisions. But the next generation and the ones after are afforded more opportunity, right? Especially if our parents did work their tail off and gave 20-30 years of their life to raising us. Why must we follow the same pattern of settling down in a 20-mile suburban life bubble? Can living be approached differently?

I know I'm not the only one challenging this. There are a lot of people exploring the world as they raise children. I've learned about them on this change in our life. We're not homeschooling our children and traveling for a year like many are doing. We're giving them structure and nesting enough to create a home base here in Tirana. Our rented apartment isn't so big that we can't all clean and care for it without the help of others. The pace of our life isn't so busy that we need to pay the premium price of convenience or throw spontaneity out the window. Sure, we aren't making the big six figure paychecks, but it's a more modest living that feels like we're living. And accessible travel is more affordable outside of the US. This new approach (I often call it an experiment) has changed the dynamic in our family and as an observer I like what I'm seeing. The great reprogramming.

It doesn't stop the dialogue or fear that this life choice may put less in savings; leaving us less prepared for the big retirement age and we may be a burden to our children someday. However, I am not of the mentality that I'm working towards retirement. That retirement is when the good stuff starts for me. Because even if you earn a middle to upper class income and pay into a retirement, the social security and retirement checks will be a tough budget to live on IF your body is able to go out and play in the world. And don't get divorced and lose half of your savings to lawyers which leaves you with even less. The price of living will be too expensive and let's face it. It will never stop climbing. This means you take on odd jobs here and there or work later on in life; both keep you stationary once again.

I am not suggesting I have all the answers or that my life choices are any better than anyone else's. My brain is simply telling me that there are more ways to live when mainstream school of thought makes me think otherwise. I guess you could say I "settled down" for 11ish years since Jackson was born. I started paying into my 401K at 19, got married at 24, started a family at 28, which led to a life insurance policy and an expanded financial portfolio. We went on to purchase the family home, after the starter home, and as I was promoted to make more money we spent more money. We bought into season tickets, luxury items, and ticked all the boxes for family traditions. The kids were active in sports and creative activities. We were surrounded by a loving community of family and friends. We carried two big car payments and I even wanted to buy a bigger house before we left. We were living the American Dream. Hook line and sinker.

I don't presume to know how my story ends or what next month or next year will bring, but I do feel hopeful. Getting sidetracked from the life I was living, allowed me to understand what makes me feel alive. I now feel less stuck. Positive energy is flowing even in the moments of being homesick and missing the people we love. This change isn't easy. It takes guts, perseverance, patience, but I am seeing the act of living in a whole new light. My parenting is still large and in full effect in this stripped-down version of myself. I am incredibly proud of doing this in front of and for my children. The world feels less separated from me and shedding fear and guilt of my past becomes easier with each day I live. I'm healing. Lessons from this experience are stacked up high and I can't wait to carry them forward. Understanding your place in the world can offer such peace to your spirit. And I have discovered that my place is everywhere.

Epilogue

* Day 313 *

My dreams are getting more and more intense as our trip home gets closer. Thank goodness, I'm no longer working and can take my time getting the day started. Must. Make. Coffee. With all the blinds shut, it's been in the 90s lately, there is little light in the apartment. Bare feet on the floor, I feel my muscles tense as I make my way to the kitchen. I'm sore from the dance class I gave myself yesterday. Needed it to relieve all this stress. With the updates to my company website complete and Isabel's 8th birthday fully celebrated, I can now focus on yet another moment of transition. Just me, my music, the sound of my keyboard as I type, and the fans making the curtains dance. This whole experience has come full circle.

I can't help but think back on all this has been. This place. The people we've met. The history and cultural lessons we've encountered. The sights we've seen. The impression it has made on this family and the peace in my heart that it brought me. The chance for a do over before it was too late.

The time here was a roller coaster to say the least, but there were many professional and personal moments of victory. The ups and downs had us living each day like it was our last. We covered a lot of ground and our passport stamps stacked up. In Albania: Tirana, Durrës, Shkodër, Vlorë, Cape of Rodon, Berat, Pogradec, Golem, Dajti Mountain National Park, Ksamil, Sarandë, Blue Eye, Butrint, Gjirokastër. Outside of the country included: Italy: Florence, Cinque Terra, Pisa, Montenegro: Budva, Kotor, Kolasin, Croatia: Dubrovnik, Ston, Mali Ston, Macedonia: Ohrid, Bay of Bones, St. Naum, Greece: Corfu, Meteora, Kosovo: Pristina. We even had visits from childhood friends, and my mom accompanied my aunt on her first trip to Europe which included a week with us for my 40th birthday. Sean's dad and stepmom added Albania and Macedonia to their Italy and Croatia trip. Seeing Dan fall in love with the Balkans and discover he is still very capable of travel was a special treat. Both Sean and I got closer to our parents through them coming here and our own family of four has never felt tighter. Not sure of another situation that could have done the same.

Adding my recent work to my portfolio, created a sense of pride. ALIST launched in Tirana, Albania and it will always be the place I started a new path. Leading the professional training in Italy was a highlight and then to go on to promote a successful Photo Festival for DMO Albania and help a local branding agency expand their creative thinking and operations, has been quite a ride. Working in an environment, where my language isn't the first language spoken by my co-workers, was illuminating. It's tough. We have traveled to countries for a week or two at a time and no English was spoken. Living and working here for the last year gave me an insight like no other. How isolating it can be. Disconnected. How it's on you to figure it out and be confident in yourself. How your survival instincts kick in and you have to assume everyone loves you. As I sat in meetings fully spoken in Albanian, my mind would wonder what it was like when my Filipino grandparents came over. Or all the others that immigrate to the US. Assimilation in a new land takes a special kind of strength. Finding work when you speak a different language is even harder. Lucky for me, my co-workers knew a little English, but not enough to get my sarcastic humor or slang way of speaking. It was difficult to fully connect, but I became highly aware of body language, facial expressions and tone. Plus, hand gestures and pointing are great fillers for lack of vocabulary.

Working internationally for the first time was like going back to school. It taught me so much. About myself. About others. About what success looks like to me and how the definition is ever changing. This year, success was knowing when to tap out and make the changes I desperately needed to continue. And I now know this consulting path is viable. It gives me the flexibility I need at home and feeds my analytical brain. I am working for myself and creativity is awake in me once again. I am back to the 20-something girl who writes, dances, and holds down a consulting gig. It's good to see her staring back at me in the mirror. My stars have aligned.

Of course, I am her with the added bonus of a wonderful husband and two kids. Living the fast life can leave little time to discuss a life change and if there is time you're just too tired. You feel stuck. And most opt for divorce as a pathway to a different life. The slower pace of the Mediterranean (the Albanians even have a phrase Avash Avash) afforded Sean and me the energy to use almost every day to talk honestly about the life we both want. But first, I had to own the task of figuring out what I really wanted out of life. Only time with myself could give me the answer. I honestly didn't know. Most of my life was dictated by others or societal norms and I followed. I now want to live the life I know I want. Defined by me. Plus, Sean and I are on the same page for the first time in a long time. Makes it bittersweet to go home early, but it's the right thing to do. The instability of Sean working in a developing country has been exhausting and taxing on our health. Since we've arrived it's been a battle. Lured here under false pretenses and the Albanian businessman way of leading through fear of losing your job at any moment made the year a challenge. Much of the administrative staff of Sean's sister school was fired and attention to his school leadership is coming next. His boss alerted us to start planning an exit and interview for other jobs. It's a shame really. Our first and most likely last International School experience ended before it ever really began. But maybe this was the way it was meant to be.

In addition, anti-government protests have been happening almost weekly in Tirana for the past four months and last week, recordings were leaked connecting the Prime Minister to the growing drug gangs and corruption suffocating this beautiful region. The wiretaps linked him directly to the Avdylaj crime gang based in Durrës and this group even infiltrated the government with one member holding a Parliament seat. The tapes also confirm the claims that vote-buying and intimidation tactics were used in the 2017 parliamentary elections. Many claim that Rama is the ringleader of all of this. Albania is becoming Europe's first narco-state and everything that comes with that status is starting to unfold. The increased poverty and lack of choices for the resident youth are making the drug path far too attractive.

Average salaries are between 250-300 Euros a month. Bananas and avocados continue to pop up at every produce stand. I try not to think about the cocaine that was stashed with them as they traveled from Columbia to Durrës. The tension continues to get thicker and the activity more hostile with each protest. Rightfully so, people want answers and change. The whole parliament walked out, demanding the Prime Minister step down. Without an operating government, Albania is back to a dictatorship. Opposition continues to protest and as Edi Rama stays in office the EU most likely won't accept Albania. The Albanian President canceled the elections at the end of June due to threats of violence and headlines warn of a possible civil war.

I keep checking the US Embassy in Albania for any signs of an increased threat, but it still reads "normal." Between the worry of losing Sean's job and the instability of the political climate, we've decided to leave. Gillian, who's been our ever-constant friend in all this and not just because she's one of Sean's Vice Principals, was already planning to move back to her home in Vancouver, BC once the school year ends. She's offered us room in her shipping crate to get our belongings home safely. Feels very much meant to be. Meeting Gillian and the many other women I connected with is one of my many positives I'll take from this experience. I am happy she and I will still get to live close to one another and for me to have a friend close by who understands the year the Maileys lived in Albania. Once we're home, we'll road trip north to collect everything, but we can't go home just yet due to tax purposes. We have a few more weeks of travel to close out this wild adventure before Sean starts his new position and we move into our new apartment back in Oregon. We're heading back to Ireland and France to visit friends and to show the kids two places that mark the love story of their parents.

Sadness comes over me when I think about the Albanians who have no choice. Who feel stuck and most are in fact physically stuck. This is their home. Incredible tradition and gorgeous landscapes are getting overrun by greed at a time when joining the EU felt plausible. The organized crime is infecting the economic and political progress of the country. It's a slippery slope and similar fraud can be found in the local businesses. Civil unrest seems imminent in Tirana and the EU appears to be on shaky ground too. The US and Europe don't want to get involved with the Albanian politics, but who is going to help the citizens? The male-centric culture doesn't treat women well. Much of the lifestyle has felt like traveling back in time. To a simpler life. A slower life. But it also means going back to a time where human rights are lacking. Respect and dignity for your fellow man, woman, is hard to find. Equal rights aren't even a discussion and diversity isn't celebrated. As an American I have the freedom to leave when the cards don't feel fairly dealt. It gives me a heavy heart to leave my Albanian friends and especially the women I got to work alongside. On the one hand my freedom makes me grateful, but on the other hand it shows the human divide. A divide I felt in the US and a divide I feel even more as a foreigner living in a developing country. In fact, the world climate is scary whether we live here, the United States, or somewhere else. I still work on finding the bright spots and I am leaving with many. I saw and still see immense beauty in this region. I'll hold onto these memories forever. There will always be life before and after Albania.

Albania is an ancient nation with an ever-changing border and a vast history of falling down and getting back up again. It was a great place for me to do just that. I recall the letters etched into the mountains in Berat. A local 58-year-old farmer and his nephew switched the "E" and "N" in the ENVER name that served as a dedication to the dictator, Enver Hoxha. Now it reads, "NEVER." A chilling reminder to never again fall to communism. To not go backwards. Only forward. I hope this message remains both aspirational and a reflection of reality in Albania. Because we all deserve a life we want to live. Albania gave me this gift and I will NEVER forget it.